SOME POINTS OF ORDER— AND ORIGINALITY—FROM SPEAKERS AND SPEECHWRITERS.

"I dictated my talk to my secretary and told her to cross out anything she thought was dull and uninteresting.

"And so, in conclusion—"

"Before I start talking, I want to say something."

George Bernard Shaw, asked to make some remarks on the sexual relations between men and women, rose and said, "Ladies and gentlemen, it gives me great pleasure," and then sat down.

Some thoughts on brevity or the lack of it—

- If a thing goes without saying, let it.
- The speaker who rises to the occasion should know when to sit down.
- The reason we make a long story short is so that we can tell another.
- What many orators lack in depth they give you in length.

Also by Eric W. Johnson
Published by Ivy Books:

A TREASURY OF HUMOR

A TREASURY OF HUMOR II

Eric W. Johnson

IVY BOOKS • NEW YORK

Ivy Books
Published by Ballantine Books
Copyright © 1994 by Eric W. Johnson

Library of Congress Catalog Card Number: 93-91733

ISBN 0-8041-1186-3

Manufactured in the United States of America

First Edition: March 1994

10 9 8 7 6 5 4 3 2

Contents

Introduction

Humor, Laughter, and Life—and How to Use This Book

I hope that this book, a successor to my *A Treasury of Humor*, will help make your life and the lives of the people you know and meet more enjoyable and richer. Humor is a multidimensional treasure. Often, but not always, humor results in laughter. Here's what the famed Irish playwright Sean O'Casey says about it: "Laughter is wine for the soul—laughter soft, or loud and deep, tinged through with seriousness. Comedy and tragedy step through life together, arm in arm. . . . Once we can laugh, we can live. It is a hilarious declaration made by man that life is worth living.* Man is always . . . pushing toward better things; and to bring this about, a change must be made in the actual way of life; so

---

* [See story number 45 on the use of *man* or *mankind* instead of *human beings* or *humankind*.]

laughter is brought in to mock at things as they are so that they may topple down, and make room for better things to come."

However, as George Burns once said in the middle of a story, "Stop laughing and listen"—*and*, I may add, even think! But the main thing is: *enjoy*, and share your enjoyment, *and* always laugh *with*, not *at*, people.

You will see from looking at the Table of Contents that this book contains some 584 humorous stories, each numbered. Actually, a good many of the stories contain several parts, so that the total may be nearer a thousand—but who's counting? You will also see that the stories are grouped into 16 chapters. This grouping was very difficult to do because almost all of the stories are on a number of subjects of life.

Therefore, if you want to find a story on a specific subject, look in the Index. For example, story number 1, in chapter 1, "Language—Bon Mottery and Deeper," shows up in the Index under these subjects: English language; headlines; humor; language; law; nudity; obscenity; Topeka, Kansas; world languages. The Index will also help you to find again a story you enjoyed and want to use.

Please note that the Index numbers are not page numbers but *story* numbers. This enables you to find quickly just what you need.

One problem with collecting humorous stories (which I have been doing for many years) is that very often you don't know where they come from. They are passed around from person to person and become general, noncopyrightable human property. What a blessing!

So who will find this book useful and pleasing?

- anyone who wants to be entertaining
- anyone who wants to be entertained
- anyone who wants to make a point memorably
- anyone who wants to spice up a conversation
- anyone who wants to enjoy marriage more
- conference speakers
- teachers
- preachers (Yes, even preachers!)
- lawyers
- lecturers
- doctors (Yes, especially doctors)
- partygoers
- before/during/after-dinner speakers
- and anyone who enjoys the orgasmic pleasure of leading up to a laugh and then hearing it burst forth

So, dear reader of *A Treasury of Humor II*, enjoy *and share*!

Eric W. Johnson

1.

Language—Bon Mottery and Deeper

Human beings are probably the only creatures on earth who have a real sense of humor. Yes, dogs wag their tails, birds chirp and sing, cats purr and meow, and those special birds called parrots imitate. Of course, some animals may well have a sense of humor, and we humans are not clever enough to detect it.*

1. To have a real sense of humor, we need language—a highly complex form of human behavior. And English is perhaps the best language in the world for humor, since it is such a complex combination of other languages: Latin, 36%; Anglo-Saxon, 14%; Old French (before 1500), 12%; Modern French, 9%; Greek, 4.5%; Scandinavian, 2%; Spanish, 2%; Italian, 1%; other languages, 13.5%; and un-

---

*If any readers have evidence of animal humor, I beg them to send me specific examples, and possibly what I receive will make a chapter for a new book. My address is: 6110 Ardleigh St., Philadelphia, PA 19138.

known, 6%. This complexity makes possible headlines like one recently published in the Topeka, Kansas, *Capital Journal*: ANTI-NUDITY LAW TO GET CLOSER LOOK.

2. In March 1992 the movie *Memoirs of an Invisible Man* came out, starring Chevy Chase and Daryl Hannah. In reviewing the film, Neil Rosen of New York City's WIVCN said, "*Invisible Man* is a must-see!"

3. One must be careful not to use certain kinds of language in certain situations. For example, some workmen were doing some construction at a convent. They used strong and profane language, which disturbed the novices. The novices complained to the Mother Superior, who then asked the foreman to speak to the men.

Foreman: But, Mother, they're rough, tough men who use blunt language. They just call a spade a spade.

Mother Superior: That, I wouldn't mind, but they keep referring to it as a f——king shovel.

4. A Quaker lady was prudently driving her car when she was crashed into by a reckless, uncaring youth. After they had exchanged license numbers and persuaded some onlookers to act as witnesses, the Quaker said to the youth in a very mild manner: "Dear friend, I hope when thee arrives home, thy mother comes out from under the porch and bites thee."

What a tactful way of calling someone an S.O.B.!

5. The famous American orator, politician, railroad president, and Republican Senator from New York, Chauncey Depew (1834–1928), gave the nominating speeches at the Republican conventions of 1888 and 1896. Once he was seated next to a society matron who said, "Oh, Mr. Depew, I've heard of your brilliant repartee, but I must warn you that I intend to give you tit for tat!"

Depew replied, "Okay, madam. Tat!"

6. If you speak and read English, consider yourself lucky, because lots of other people do, too. Be glad that you don't live on the South Pacific Island of Vanuotu, which has a population of about 160,000 and is the size of Connecticut and Rhode Island combined. The people of Vanuotu speak 106 distinct languages. (In the whole world there are approximately 2,500 living languages.)

7. One must be careful how one uses language when communicating with people from different countries. For example, an English lady, while visiting in Switzerland, was looking for a room, and she asked the local schoolmaster to recommend places. He took her to see several rooms. She arranged to rent one and returned to England to make final preparations for the move. When she arrived home, the thought suddenly occurred to her that she had seen no "water closet" near the room, so she wrote to the schoolmaster to inquire whether there was a W.C. around. The schoolmaster asked the parish priest to help him figure out what was meant by the letters W.C. The only meaning they could find was a wayside chapel. The schoolmaster then wrote this letter to the lady:

Dear Madam:

I take great comfort in informing you that a W.C. is located nine miles from the house in the center of a beautiful grove of trees surrounded by lovely grounds.

It is capable of holding two hundred people and is open on Sundays and Thursdays only. As there are a great many tourists expected during the summer months, I would advise your ladyship to come early, although there is usually plenty of standing room. This is an unfortunate situation, especially if you are in the habit of going regularly.

8. "Going regularly" suggests emphasis on a certain part of the body. This is reinforced by a delightful linguistic mistranslation reported in James Reston's wonderful book *Deadline* (Random House, 1991). During World War II, Adlai Stevenson (1900–1965) served in the Navy, supervising U.S. arms shipments to the Soviet Union. A Soviet official complained that the U.S.A. was behind in its shipments, but Stevenson said that it was because the Soviets were behind in giving a schedule of their needs. The Russian said, "I have not come here to talk about my behind but about your behind."

9. As many U.S. tourists know, although Mexico is a delightful, beautiful, and historic country to visit, tourists often suffer from stomach problems caused by impure water. This led one fine Mexican restaurant to post a large sign by the front door reading: THE MANAGER HAS PERSONALLY PASSED ALL THE WATER SERVED HERE.

10. One of the delights of language is punning. Bill and Eleanor have increased the joy of their 55-year-old marriage by Bill's puns. He made his most famous one when some bats had made their home in the peak of their log cabin in Canada. When Eleanor complained about the mess the bats' droppings made on the porch floor, Bill's comment was, "Yup, it's a real bat shituation."

11. According to the Civil Code of California, "Superfluity does not vitiate." When asked by a witness in court what that means, a judge explained: "Shut up!"

12. Even the great political orator Sir Winston Churchill (1874–1965) was guilty at times of using overelaborate phrases. Once in a debate he admitted that he might have been guilty of a "terminological inexactitude." His opponent, Joseph Chamberlain, replied, "I prefer the ugly little English three-letter word: l-i-e."

13. Noah Webster (1758–1843) was for many years the chief authority on the English language. His greatest work was *The American Dictionary of the English Language*.

One day Webster's wife came into the pantry and caught him in the act of embracing the chambermaid. "Noah!" she said. "I am surprised!"

"No, my pet," he replied. "You are amazed. It is we who are surprised."

Famous authors are geniuses at expressing their outrage when they are criticized or their work is rejected.

14. Robert Burns (1759–1796), the Scottish poet and author of "Flow Gently, Sweet Afton," "Auld Lang Syne," and "Comin' Thro' the Rye," in 1791 wrote this to a critic:

"Thou eunuch of language: thou butcher, imbruing thy hands in the bowels of orthography: thou arch-heretic in pronunciation: thou pitch-pipe of affected emphasis: thou carpenter, mortising the awkward joints of jarring sentence: thou squeaking dissonance of cadence: thou pimp of gender: thou scape-gallows from the land of syntax: thou scavenger of mood and tense: thou murderous accoucheur of infant learnings: thou *ignis fatuus*, misleading the steps of benighted ignorance: thou pickle-herring in the puppet-show of nonsense."

15. D. H. Lawrence (1885–1930), author of the famous *Lady Chatterly's Lover*, was furious when his first novel, *Sons and Lovers*, was rejected by a publisher. He wrote to his friend Edward Garnett: "Curse the blasted, jelly-boned swines, the slimy, the belly-wriggling invertebrates, the miserable sodding rutters, the flaming sods, the sniveling, dribbling, dithering, palsied, pulse-less lot that make up England today. They've got the white of egg in their veins and their spunk is that watery it's a marvel they can breed."

16. We've been looking at examples of the apt use of language. How about its unapt—or should I say *inept*?—use? *New York Times* reporter Maria Odum starts an article titled "If It Talks Like a Lawyer, There May Yet Be a Cure" (June 5, 1992) by asking, "Why does a Georgia state court subpoena warn: 'Herein fail not on pain of $300.' Why can't it simply say: 'If you do not appear in court, you will be fined $300'?"

To find examples of "legalese," or "gobbledegook," or "legaldegook," a fine source is the reports of opinions and decisions of lawyers and judges cited in federal courts and departments of the New York Supreme Court. Here are four items of legaldegook. Can you say what they mean?

1. "Matters should be held in abeyance pending the meeting in order to determine whether the facts there adduced will warrant a further extension." 2. "The administrator has ample power now to frame the remedy to take into consideration any unconscionable delay in bringing a complaint to the attention of the administrator." 3. "That dicta, however, is clearly inapposite." 4. "Unilateral nullification of the terms and conditions of the expiring agreement absent bona fide impasse is prohibited."

O.K., what they mean in plain English (no gook), as translated by Odum: 1. "We should wait to act until we see what we find out at our next meeting, where we might decide to put it off again." 2. "The administrator has the power to decide how to handle late complaints." 3. "You are citing the wrong thing." 4. "One party cannot leave the contract early without a good reason."

17. Perhaps it's all right for lawyers and judges to use strange words. It's one of the ways they make their living—by guiding clients out of the gobbledegook wilderness. If there were no wilderness, few guides would be needed.

But how about schoolteachers? Surely they should know how to write, and therefore teach, plain—or at least effective—English. Well, here are four examples of our language, written by English teachers:

- It is true that some rhetorics have denied their imbrication in ideology, doing so in the name of a disinterested scientism. More recently the discussion of the relation between ideology and rhetoric has taken a new turn. Ideology is here foregrounded and problematized in a way that situates rhetoric within ideology, rather than ideology within rhetoric.

- There is a need for conscientization to counter the interferences to critical thought in daily life.
- Concretely my class's study of hamburgers not only involved English and philosophy in our use of writing, reading, and conceptual analysis, but it also included economics in the study of the commodity relations which bring hamburgers to market, history and sociology in an assessment of what the everyday diet was like before the rise of the hamburger, and health science in terms of the nutritional value of the ruling burger.
- You students and your ancestors have been coming to the land now called the United States for millennia.

Perhaps four examples are enough. They make us recognize the truth that George Orwell (1903–1950) expressed in his *Politics and the English Language*: "A mass of Latin words falls upon the facts like soft snow, blurring the outlines and covering up all the details."

18. Before we get into the problems of Latin, I should point out that English is the most useful language in the world to know how to speak, read, and understand. Here are some facts:

- English is used by one of every seven human beings on earth.
- Half of the world's books are written in English.
- The majority of international phone calls are made in English.
- Over 60% of the world's radio programs are broadcast in English.
- Over 70% of international mail is written in English.
- Eighty percent of all computer text is stored in English.
- English has the world's largest vocabulary—about two million words.

And yet English is a strange language. For example:

- sharp and blunt speech are the same;
- overlook and oversee are opposites;
- your nose runs and your feet smell;
- a vegetarian eats vegetables, but what does a humanitarian eat?;
- yesterday the teacher taught, but last Sunday the preacher didn't praught;
- there are no peas in peanuts, no pine or apple in pineapple, no mush or room in mushroom, no grape in grapefruit, no butter in buttermilk, no egg in eggplant, no bread in shortbread;
- a woman can man a station, but a man can't woman one;
- a man can father a movement, but a woman can't mother one;

- a king rules a kingdom, but queens don't rule a queendom.

19. Isn't it strange that the words *ruly, ert, ept, ane, sipid, and mune* do not exist in English, whereas their negatives *unruly, inert, inept, inane, insipid, and immune* do?

20. And, of course, English spelling presents problems. An examination question asked why "psychic" is spelled with a *p*. One student who really didn't know felt that he should at least give it a try, so he wrote, "It pcertainly does pseem psomewhat psilly."

21. It's strange to me that so many educators and teachers have such reverence for Latin and the usefulness of studying it. It would be a better use of students' time for them to learn a number of Latin roots, prefixes, and suffixes in order to increase their vocabulary. As for Latin grammar, it is almost totally different from the grammar of English, Latin being based mainly on the *form* of words, while English is more based on *word order*.

However, the Roman Catholic Church is often a loyal user of Latin, and one of the Church's problems is to keep Latin up-to-date, which is the responsibility of the Vatican's Latinatus Foundation. Here is the Latin version of four relatively modern English words: ENGLISH: *slot machine*; LATIN: *sphaerilu-*

dium electricum nomismate actum. ENGLISH: *disco-theque*; LATIN: *orbium phonographiscorum theca.* ENGLISH: *dishwasher*, LATIN: *escariorum lavator.* ENGLISH: *cover girl*; LATIN: *exterioris paginae puella.*

22. Another problem with Latin was faced by a Catholic who was studying to be a monk. Latin is often used in the Church and in Catholic documents. Therefore, the monk-to-be had to learn to count in Latin. He had no trouble with the first five numbers—*unus, duo, tres, quattuor, quinque*—but when he came to the number six, anguish appeared on his face. In Latin "six" is *sex*.

23. As I'm sure most of my readers know, the word *primate*, a word of Latin origin, can mean apes, monkeys (or even human beings), and also the bishop or archbishop of a church. Archbishop Michael Peers, primate of the Anglican Church of Canada, was astonished to receive a letter from the Wisconsin Regional Primate Research Center. But his secretary, a priest, replied quite adequately, thus: "I think the primates in your study are perhaps a different species. While it is true that our primate occasionally enjoys bananas, I have never seen him walk with his knuckles on the ground or scratch himself publicly under the armpits."

The Center replied very knowledgeably thus: "We

have strayed on this occasion from the arboreal to the spiritual."

24. The Inuit people (we generally call them Eskimos) speak a language called Inuktitut. Missionaries have had great problems translating the Bible into that language. Inuktitut has no word for donkey, sheep, or horse. (However, it has thirty words for snow.) So what to do with the term "lamb of God"? The translation is: "God's special thing that looks like a caribou calf."

Recently, however, the Inuits are learning more words. *Sheep* is *sheepi*, and so forth. However, *donkey* is still "the thing with big ears."

25. In Forrest Carter's wonderful book *The Education of Little Tree* (Delacorte Press, 1976), he tells about the Cherokees of the Southwest and explains the special greeting that Native Americans use with "white men":

"As to folks saying, 'How!' and then laughing when they see an Indian, Granpa said it all come about over a couple of hundred years. He said every time the Indian met a white man, the white man commenced to ask him: *how* are you feeling, or *how* are your people, or *how* are you getting along, or *how* is the game where you come from, and so on. He said the Indian come to believe that the white man's favorite subject was *how*; and so, being polite, when he met the white man, he figured he would just say *how*, and then let the son of a bitch talk about whichever *how* he wanted to. Granpa said people laughing at that was laughing at an Indian who was trying to be courteous and considerate."

Some assuring examples of language come from instructions or documents written for English-speaking customers by non-English-speaking writers. Here are three examples:

26. From a Taiwanese modem manufacturer: "Once you have the necessary items, plug the RS-232 connector on the back side of the Mini Modem 2400 into the RS-232C connector on your computer, printer, or terminal, then screw up."

27. From a Chinese manufacturer of alarm clocks: "When the Basic Time corresponds to the preset Alarm Time, the alarm is generated. The Alarm tune will automatically cease after 1 minute working. If you have a depress on 'SNOOZE' while it is alarmed, the loud will stop immediately and loud for another 8 minutes after having this 'SNOOZE' 8 minutes and so on. However, alarm will not effect if it has lasted for fully 8 minutes unless the second correspondence that is to say after 24 hours."

28. From a Venezuelan travel brochure: "In this Expedition you will know the highets waterfall in the worlf. From Canaima, trough the Sabana, the Jungle and the rivers Carrao & Churun, you'll enjoy one of the biggets emotions in this life. All the facihties Camp. Guides an Natives, all experts will bring you trough troubles waters, just where a few have made it. Be you one of them, Meals ni open fire never taste so goo. DAYS. To arrange with the group."

But it's not only foreigners who mess up the English language. Consider the following:

29. A woman speaking about a person who was expelled from a club said, "They dismembered her."

30. A passenger said to a city bus driver, "Please proscrastinate me at Fourth and Arch Streets."

"Huh?" said the driver. "I don't get you."

"Well," said the passenger, "procrastinate means to put off, doesn't it? So, driver, procrastinate me where I told you to."

31. A sailor was asked, "Do you have any pornographic literature?"

"Pornographic literature?!" he replied. "Hell, no! I don't even have a pornograph."

32. A young student was trying to earn some money over the summer. He knocked at the door of a rich man's house and asked if there was anything he could do.

"Yes," the man replied, "you can paint the porch. The paint and brushes are in the garage."

Three hours later, the student came back and reported, "Well, it's all painted, but I gotta tell you, that's not a Porsche; it's a Ferrari."

33. Members of the Ancient Order of Hibernians of Johnstown, Pennsylvania, were discussing whether to buy a chandelier for their club. After a good deal of argument a fellow got up and said, "I don't think we should spend a lot of money on something like that. There's not one of us who knows how to play it."

34. A farmer gave his neighbor a lift into town. His truck was old and almost springless and the country roads were very rough, so there was a lot of jouncing. As they finally stopped at their destination, the neighbor said, "I really do appreciate this. I hope someday I'll be able to recuperate."

Mixed metaphors are another way of messing up the language.

35. At a public hearing about federal spending a citizen stood up and shouted, "Senators, if we don't stop shearing the wool off the goose that lays the golden egg, we're going to pump the well dry!" Message clear, no?

Sometimes the misuse of vocabulary, grammar, or spelling can get us into trouble:

36. A headline in the *Boston Globe*: LAW STUDENTS START DRIVE FOR MANDATORY VOLUNTEERISM.

37. News item from the Yeovil, U.K., *Western Gazette*: "The first swallow has arrived at Devizes. It was spotted by Police Constable John Cooke, of Seend, whose hobby is birdwatching, sitting wet and bedraggled on telephone wires."

38. *Fifth-grade girl to teacher*: "I ain't got no pencil."

Teacher: "It's 'I don't have a pencil'; 'You don't have a pencil'; 'We don't have any pencils'; 'They don't have any pencils.' Is that clear?"

Girl: "No. What happened to all them pencils?"

39. Charles-Augustin Sainte-Beuve (1804–1869) was a famous literary critic and historian. Once he got into a violent argument with another writer, who finally said, "I challenge you to a duel. You may have the choice of weapons."

"I choose spelling," said Sainte-Beuve. "You're dead!"

The pronunciation of letters or words or phrases can give us pleasure or get us into trouble.

40. A father had a strong argument with his teenage daughter. It ended like this:

Daughter: "It's a mute point."

Father: "No it's not, and I think you mean moot point."

Daughter: "No, Pop, I mean *mute* point. I don't want to talk about it anymore."

41. A young student had trouble pronouncing the letter *R*. Therefore, his teacher gave him this sentence to practice on: "Robert gave Richard a rap in the ribs for roasting the rabbit so rare."

After a few days the teacher asked him to repeat the sentence. The boy said, "Bob gave Dick a poke in the side for not cooking the bunny enough."

42. George Bernard Shaw (1856–1950) got great pleasure in using language exactly, and also, sometimes, in subtly putting people down. Once the historian and military strategist Sir Basil Henry Liddell Hart said to Shaw, "Did you know that 'sumac' and 'sugar' are the only two words in English that begin with *su* and are pronounced *shu*?"

Shaw replied, "Sure."

43. And where you accent a phrase can make a great difference. For example: "*wise* guy" and "wise *guy*."

44. It is commonly understood that a proverb is a brief popular epigram or maxim. How is it, then, that so many proverbs contradict others? Here are two examples:

(1) "Absence makes the heart grow fonder."
(2) "Out of sight, out of mind."

(1) "He who hesitates is lost."
(2) "Look before you leap."

45. O.K., now to *mankind*. For years I have refused to use the word because, after all, the human race is made up of man and woman. So I have conscientiously used the word *humankind*, a word that Ronald Reagan, I think, first made popular, even though it originated in 1645. And when I looked in the dictionary I saw that *woman* derived from the Old English *wifman, wife* plus *man*.

But now I know better. Actually, in Old English (or Anglo-Saxon) the word "man" was genderless and referred to all humans. And the Old English for a male person (perdaughter?) was *waepman*, and for a female, *wifman*.

And it's interesting that in 1776, when Thomas Jefferson (1743–1826) wrote in the Declaration of Independence that "all men are created equal," he was not being sexist. At that time "men" often meant "human beings." That very same year, 1776, the Scottish philosopher and historian David Hume (1711–1776) referred in his work to "all men, both male and female."

Well, all of this talk about female and male, women and men, leads very naturally, if not logically, into our next chapter.

2.

Marriage—a Complicated Human Condition

The first sentence of the entry *marriage* in *The New Columbia Encyclopedia* (1975 edition) defines it as a "socially sanctioned union of one or more men with one or more women." Does that sound simple or complicated? Think about it as you read the following item.

46. There are a number of terms describing marriage. Here are a few:

- *exogamy*: the obligation to marry outside your own group
- *endogamy*: the obligation to marry within your own group
- *arranged marriage*: where a matchmaker is employed by the families. Sometimes, quite a while ago and especially among Slavic peoples and South American Indians, the future husband and wife were pledged in childhood, occasionally even before birth.
- *place of residence*: There are three choices:

(1) *patrilocal*—with or near the husband's family;

(2) *matrilocal*—with or near the wife's family;

(3) *neolocal*—independent of either family.

- *monogamy*—one wife and one husband
- *polygyny*—one husband and several wives
- *polyandry*—one wife and several husbands
- *sororate marriage*—one husband married to two or more sisters (not his own sisters—that would be *incest*)
- *levirate marriage*—a widow marrying her late husband's brother
- *common-law marriage*—when a couple agrees to live together as married, but without any religious or legal ceremony.

We could go on, but you can see that marriage, even in its definitions, is a complicated form of human behavior.

Most of the following stories about marriage are about neolocal, legal marriages.

47. Mark Twain (1835–1910) was interested in, and humorous about, all kinds of human behavior, including marriage. (He married Olivia Langdon in 1870.) Once he was discussing the question of polygamy with a Mormon friend. The discussion became heated, and the Mormon finally challenged Twain with this question: "Can you tell me of a single passage of Scripture whereon polygamy is forbidden?"

"That's easy," Twain replied. " 'No man can serve two masters' " (Matt. 6.24).

48. A common statement is that "marriages are made in heaven." However, most married couples would agree that the maintenance work is done down here.

49. Speaking of maintenance work, let me report that a man and his wife argued so much that they finally saw a marriage counselor. The man said to a friend, "We still argue, but now we call it sharing."

50. Another story about the necessity of maintenance. A famous Shakespearian actress, Mrs. Patrick Campbell, was once asked by a man, "Why do you suppose it is that women so utterly lack a sense of humor?"

Mrs. Campbell replied, "God arranged it on purpose so that we would love you men instead of laughing at you."

51. George Bernard Shaw, the Irish-born British playwright and critic, wrote a letter to the English actress Dame Ellen Terry revealing his attitude about marriage and the perfect mate: "Do you know a reasonably healthy woman of about 60, accustomed to plain vegetarian cooking, and able to read and write enough to forward letters when her husband is away, but otherwise uneducated?"

52. While we're under the Irish influence, consider this event. Two Irishmen, Robin and Paddy, met at a pub. They had not seen each other for many years. After cordial greetings, they each ordered a pint, and then Robin said, "Tell me now, Paddy, did you ever marry?"

"I did," replied Paddy, "and my wife's an angel."

"Sure and you're a lucky man," said Robin. "Mine's still with me."

53. But there are men who very much like being married. One of these is a young father who was riding a bicycle with his toddler well strapped into a seat behind him. On the back of the child's seat was a sign: "My dad's single. To contact him call 555-3238."

In married relationships, money is quite often a problem. Consider the following:

54. *George to Larry*: "In the past, you know, a man wondered if he could afford to get married."

Larry: "Yes, and so?"

George: "Now a man wonders if he can get along without a working wife."

55. Emily loved Rick, but she worried about all the

money he so rashly spent when they went out together. She asked her friend Becky, "How can I stop Rick from spending so much money on me?"

"Marry him!" Becky replied.

"Sleeping together" can have its problems.

56. An anonymous person sent me this couplet:

Heading the list of the people who try us
    Are husbands who blissfully sleep on the bias.

57. This short rhyme describes another marital sleeping problem:
    Some like it cold, some like it hot.
    Some freeze while others smother.
    And by some fiendish, fatal plot
    They marry one another.

My wife and I, happily married for nearly forty-five years, have the same problem. She always, except in hot weather, has a doubled blanket on her side of the bed. Even a dual-control electric blanket doesn't do the trick—too much lateral leakage. We call it "thermal incompatibility."

58. A woman went to a marriage counselor to get help with her marital problems. The counselor asked her some questions.

Counselor: "Do you wake up grumpy in the morning?"

Woman: "No, I let him sleep."

59. A grouchy-looking wife said to a grumpy-looking husband when he came home from work, "Look, let's make a deal. You don't tell me about your day, and I won't tell you about mine."

60. A wise person, Pauline Thomason, said, "Love is blind. Marriage is the eye-opener."

61. An attractive, able Quaker spinster was asked by a member of her Meeting, "Agnes, how is it that thee never married?"

Agnes smiled at the questioner and replied, "Well, thee knows, it takes a mighty good husband to be better than none."

62. The husband was a workaholic and often stayed very late at the office. One night he got home at 12:30 and tried to crawl gently into bed. It didn't work; his wife woke up and said, "You've got to learn to alphabetize."

"I don't understand," he replied.

She explained, "*Wife* comes before *work*."

For a change of pace—and age—let's consider marriage between the very young.

63. A three-year-old boy and a five-year-old girl were playing house. Hand in hand, they knocked at the door of a neighbor's home. The neighbor opened the door, smiled, and said, "Yes, what may I do for you?"

The girl said, "We're playing house. This is my husband, and I am his wife. Can we come in?"

"Why, of course. Do come in," replied the woman. She was so enchanted by the act that she offered them lemonade and cookies.

"Thank you!" said the boy, and they each accepted cookies and a tall glass of lemonade.

A few minutes later, the woman said, "Would you like another glass?"

"No thank you," said the girl. "We have to go now. My husband wet his pants."

More marriage problems:

64. A husband was talking to another husband, and one said, "I understand they've created a new product that lessens a man's sexual urges."

"So what else is new?" replied the other. "I married one twenty-five years ago."

65. A health education teacher was giving an evening course in sex and marriage. It was for married couples. The teacher stressed the importance of monogamy. She also stressed the danger of sexually transmitted diseases. After one class she distributed an anonymous questionnaire asking the class about their safe-sex practices. One student replied, "My wife and I don't worry about sexually transmitted diseases. We practice monotony."

66. A man said to his friend at the bar, "For twenty years my wife and I were ecstatically happy."

The bartender overheard and asked, "Then what happened?"

"We met," the man replied.

67. A young man, Jules, fell deeply in love with a young woman, Ida. He finally went to Ida's father to ask for his blessing. The father said, "So you want to become my son-in-law, do you?"

Jules replied, "No, sir, I really don't. But I want to marry your daughter, so I don't see how I can avoid it."

68. A young man on a cruise ship looked across the deck and saw this beautiful woman staring at him. Walking over to her, he said, "I notice you've been looking in my direction; is anything the matter?"

She blushed a little and said, "You remind me of my first husband."

"Really? And did he pass away?"

"No."

"Oh! Then you're divorced?"

"No. I've never been married."

69. Someone said to the British poet Alfred, Lord Tennyson that it was too bad that Thomas Carlyle, the great English author, hadn't married someone other than Jane Baillie Welsh because Thomas and Jane were so incompatible.

"No," replied Tennyson, "by any other arrangement *four* people would have been unhappy instead of two."

70. The wife of a great Quaker teacher of mine was delightfully and realistically humorous about marriage. She was a strong character. After a long marriage, her husband died. A year or two later, as she talked about her marriage, I asked her, "Did you ever consider divorce?"

"No, Eric," she replied. "Murder maybe, but never divorce."

71. When the conservative, Catholic English author G. K. Chesterton was told that in the United States it was possible to get a divorce on grounds of incompatibility, he observed, "If that is true, I find it remarkable that there are *any* marriages left in the United States."

Well, there are some marriages left in the United States, and a few of them nearly perfect. (However, what could be more boring than "We've been married for thirty-five years and never had a cross word"?)

Now consider the following worse than "cross words."

72. Mr. Horton was being tried for throwing his wife out of their seventeenth-floor apartment. The judge asked, "Why did you do it?"

Mr. Horton answered, "I forgot that we no longer live on the first floor."

73. Mrs. Mohler was being tried for the murder of her third husband. A lawyer asked, "What happened to your first husband?"

"He died of mushroom poisoning," said Mrs. Mohler.

"How about your second husband?" asked the lawyer.

"He died of mushroom poisoning, too," replied Mrs. Mohler.

"Well, then," asked the lawyer, "what about your third husband?"

Mrs. Mohler replied, "He died of brain concussion."

The lawyer asked, "Why did that happen?"

Mrs. Mohler paused, and then said, "He didn't like mushrooms."

74. And here are three marital comments:

- *Wife to husband*: "*I'm* stupid? What about you? You married me, didn't you?"
- *Husband to wife*: "Can't you just say we've been married for twenty-four years instead of 'almost a quarter of a century'?"
- *Wife to husband*: "I don't mind your little half-truths, but you keep telling me the wrong half."

75. Judith Martin, in her stimulating, practical, and funny book *Miss Manners' Guide To the Turn-of-the-Millennium* (Pharos Books, N.Y., 1989), writes:

"The world is chock-full of interesting and curious things. The point of courtship and marriage is to secure someone with whom you wish to go hand in hand through this source of entertainment, each making discoveries, and then sharing some and merely reporting others. Anyone who tries to compete with the entire world, demanding to be someone's sole source of interest and attention, is asking to be classified as a bore. 'Why don't you ever want to talk to me?' will probably never start a satisfactory marital conversation. 'Guess what?' will probably never fail."

76. "What in heaven's name happened to you?" exclaimed Mr. Grant when his wife came into the living room with her head bristling with curlers.

Mrs. Grant replied, "I just set my hair."

"Oh," said Mr. Grant. "And what time does it go off?"

77. A friend of mine from West Branch, Iowa, has an eight-year-old daughter, Jennifer. One afternoon she was playing in the backyard with some neighborhood children, all girls. She and another girl were performing a mock wedding ceremony. Yet another girl, Christina, was acting as the minister. As Jennifer's mother listened, sight unseen, she heard Christina reciting the usual vows this way: "Do you take this man to be your awfully wedded husband?"

78. Two men were discussing the infidelities of one of their office colleagues. Said one man, "I don't know how he gets away with it. The only thing I've ever done behind my wife's back is to zip her up."

79. *Mr. Jacobson to Mr. Conner*: "How's your wife?" *Mr. Conner*: "Compared to what?"

80. Wife to husband: "Wrinkles are easy to ignore if you read between the lines."

81. Monty and Mabel Warner were an elderly couple who had been very happily married for over fifty years. One morning when they woke up, Mabel said, "Monty, there's something I'd just love to have right now in bed."

"Tell me exactly what it is," replied Monty, with an attentive-looking smile, "and I'll get it."

"Well," said Mabel, "I'd like a bowl of vanilla ice cream with some chocolate syrup on top."

"Great!" said Monty. "I'll be back in a minute. Just lie there."

"Wait, Monty," said Mabel. "On top of the chocolate syrup, I want some whipped cream, *and* ... do you think you can remember all this? Maybe you'd better write it down."

"No, it's O.K. I'll remember," assured Monty. "*And* ... ?"

"And on top of the whipped cream, two sweet red cherries," Mabel finished.

Monty went down to the kitchen and about fifteen minutes later came back to the bedroom and handed Mabel a ham sandwich. She took a good bite, and then frowned.

"Monty!" she said. "You forgot the mustard."

82. An over-eighty female friend of mine wrote me a letter recently. Here's a part of it:

"I've become a little older since I saw you last, and a few changes have come into my life since then. I've become quite a frivolous old gal. I'm seeing five gentlemen a day. As soon as I wake up, Will Power helps me get out of bed. Then I go see John. Then Charlie Horse comes along. When he is here, he takes a lot of my time and attention. When he leaves Arthur Itis shows up and stays the rest of the day. He doesn't like to stay in one place, so he takes me from joint to joint. After such a busy day, I'm glad to go to bed with Ben Gay. What a life!"

83. Marriage can be a continuing joy over the years even though it doesn't always continue the utterly romantic feelings one has when falling in love. An unspoken thought many people have about their spouses might go something like this: "I will always cherish the initial misconception I had about you."

84. One woman's observation about her husband was: "Jake's idea of togetherness is when he holds the door while I take out the garbage."

85. Myra's husband complained that his wife was always nagging him. She replied, "Dear, I don't nag, I motivate."

86. Two cannibals were stirring a large pot of boiling edibles. They get into a conversation.

Cannibal one: "I really hate my mother-in-law."

Cannibal two: "Why?"

Cannibal one: "Because she's so nasty."

Cannibal two (looking into the pot): "In that case, why not just eat the potatoes and carrots?"

87. What a dull marriage it would be if husband and wife never had a cross word! Here's an example of nondullness:

Wife: "I'll admit I'm wrong if you'll admit I'm right."
Husband: "O.K. You go first."
Wife: "I'm wrong."
Husband: "You're right."

We'll end this chapter on a semiserious note.

88. Richard Crashaw (1613?–1649) was the son of an ardent Puritan clergyman. He converted to Catholicism. This English poet wrote in Greek, Latin, and English. Two of his books are *Steps To the Temple* and *Delights of the Muses*. He wrote this epitaph for himself and his wife.

> To these whom death again did wed
> This grave's the second marriage-bed.
> For though the hand of fate could force
> 'Twixt soul and body a divorce,
> It could not sever man and wife,
> Because they both lived but one life.
> Peace, good reader, do not weep;
> Peace, the lovers are asleep.

And so, not to the next life but to the next chapter, the subject of which is sex.

3.

Sex

The ordering of chapters 2 (Marriage), 3 (Sex), and 4 (Families and Children) gave me a bit of trouble, and I settled it on the basis of a Quaker experience.

89. The Society of Friends (Quakers) carefully put together a book called *Faith and Practice*. It suggests (strongly) to members how they should conduct their lives. In 1972 the Philadelphia Yearly Meeting was struggling to agree on how to order the various sections. A hot question was where to make the section on "Sexuality," a new section. Finally a lively and weighty Friend made a suggestion that satisfied everyone: It should be placed between "Marriage" and "Home and Family." (Consider the consequences of placing it *before* marriage!)

90. One night after dinner, a small boy walked into the kitchen and asked, "Mom, what's sex?"

His mother, a very enlightened parent, said, "Let's go back to your room and I'll tell you."

They did. Mom delivered a good explanation. When she was done, she said, "Now, do you have any questions?"

"Yeah," said her son, pointing to his school enrollment card. "How can I get all that stuff in this one itty-bitty square?"

91. A lawyer asked a reluctant witness, "Is it true, miss, that you are a prostitute?"

"That's my business," replied the witness.

"I see," said the lawyer. "Well, please tell the court, what are your hobbies?"

92. A gorgeous, sexy, young woman was walking through a cocktail lounge. Her eye was caught by a very attractive man, sitting alone. She said, "Hello, handsome. I'll do anything you want for $200."

"Wonderful," said the man. "Paint my house."

93. Sometimes young children get a certain amount of sex education at home, and that's fine, but it doesn't explain everything, as these true examples show:

- A four-year-old girl was looking at a cow. Then she asked her father, "Dad, why do cows have four penises?"
- Another slightly older kid observed a bull having

an erection. He asked his mother, "Why does that cow have five legs?"

94. Norris was complaining to his friend Steve about a headache. Steve said, "Norris, when I have a headache I go home and make love to my beautiful wife, and my headache leaves immediately."

A short time thereafter, Norris and Steve met again. Norris said, "I followed your advice, Steve, and my headache cleared up promptly. And, by the way, you have a beautiful home, too."

95. Dr. Warner and his wife got into a heated exchange of words during breakfast. Finally he shouted, "You aren't so good in bed either!"

With that, he got up and angrily went off to his office. But by midmorning, Dr. Warner began to feel bad about what he'd said, so he called home to make amends. The phone rang and rang, and finally Mrs. Warner answered, "Hello?"

"What took you so long to answer?"

"I was in bed," replied Mrs. Warner.

"What were you doing in bed this late?" the doctor asked.

Mrs. Warner replied, "Getting a second opinion."

96. A farmer and his wife were lying in bed one night. He started caressing his wife's bottom. While doing this, he said, "You know, if this would only lay eggs, we could get rid of the chickens."

Then he started caressing her breasts and said, "If these would only give milk, we could get rid of our cows."

After a few moments, the wife started caressing the farmer. Then she said, "You know, if this would only get hard more often, we could get rid of your farmhand."

97. During World War II in London there was a lack of sugar. A rather practical lady used to stick whatever cubes of sugar she could find in the top of her dress whenever she ate at a restaurant.

One day she returned from lunch, sugar cubes in place, to find the vicar standing at her door. "Won't you come in and have a cup of tea?" she asked.

"I'd be charmed to," replied the vicar.

As he was about to drink his tea, the lady reached in her dress and offered him two lumps of sugar. He was a bit surprised, but put the sugar in his tea and started stirring. Then the lady said, "Oh, by the way, Vicar, would you like some milk?"

The vicar replied, "Madam, you wouldn't dare!"

98. "There's no solution to the world's population explosion," said a man to his friend.

"Why not?" asked his friend.

"Because," he replied, "it's so much fun lighting the fuse."

99. Quakers (Friends) seem to have taken the world's population problem personally. Although as sexual as members of any religious group, they beget rather few children. This is one of the reasons why their numbers are slowly declining.

One Quaker I know, in order to counteract this situation, has suggested a Five-*F* Committee: the Committee *F*or *F*ertility and *F*ecundity *F*or *F*riends. But another agile-minded Friend, knowing that Quakers never have enough money to pay for all the good works they get involved in, responded that it should be the *Eight-F* Committee: the Committee *F*or *F*ertility and *F*ecundity *F*or *F*riends *F*inancially *F*ixed and *F*unded.

Want to join?

For some people, various indirect means of sexual stimulation seem to have appeal. Here are two examples from different parts of New York City.

100. This notice was published May 1991 in the *Newsletter* of the Staten Island Friends of Clearwater:

Sun., May 26—6 P.M. Horseshoe Crab Mating By Moonlight—Meet at Page Ave. and Hylan Blvd. *Witness the primal orgy of these armored creatures from the deep. Bring dinner, a flashlight, and bug repellent. We'll picnic along the beach.*

101. A recent item from the *Education Program of the New York Botanical Garden*:
BOT 179 APHRODISIACS, STIMULANTS, AND THE PLANTS OF VICE.

The rich lore and history of economic botany has given humankind several species of plants which arouse passion and promote fertility. We will identify these botanicals and describe their folk uses. In addition, we will survey other plants which have had similar Dionysian connotations such as ecstasy, altered states, and intoxication, and discuss the taboos and/or rituals associated with their use. Bring lunch.

102. A friend met 80-year-old Bruce after not having seen him for a few years. They went into a bar and got into a good conversation. At one point the friend asked, "Bruce, do you still chase beautiful women?"

"Yes, I do," said Bruce, "but sometimes I forget why."

103. Mr. and Mrs. Rinehart always went to their doctor for an annual checkup. Mr. Rinehart went first. After giving him routine tests, the doctor asked, "So, in general, how are you feeling?"

"Well, Doctor, I have one problem," Rinehart said, after a moment of hesitation.

"Tell me about it. Maybe I can help," said the doctor.

"It's about sex. The first time my wife and I make

love, everything is fine, but the second time I sweat a lot."

"Hmm," said the doctor. "Let me look up some facts and I'll get back to you."

The next day, Mrs. Rinehart went for her checkup. After it was done, the doctor decided to ask about her husband's problem. "Mr. Reinhart says that the first time you make love, everything is perfect, but he perspires the second time. Have you any idea why?"

"I certainly do," she stated. "The first time is in December, and the second time is in August."

104. An 83-year-old man married a 77-year-old woman. The first night, he squeezed her hand and then turned over and went to sleep.

On the fourth night, the husband was reaching for his wife's hand, but she said, "Not tonight, dear. I have a headache."

What does sex lead to? Turn to the next chapter and see!

4.

Families and Children

One of the important elements of family life is the disciplining of children. The ideal kind of discipline is *self*-discipline, but it doesn't always work out that way.

105. At Auburn University in Alabama, there is a series of lessons on family life. The title of one session was stated in the flyer thus: DISCIPLINING CHILDREN: CONCRETE HELPS

106. A father was hanging pictures in a second-floor bedroom. His six-year-old son, Greg, was watching him. In the living room, Greg's mother was reading a book. Suddenly the mother heard Greg coming downstairs crying loudly.

."What's the matter?" asked the mother.

"Daddy was hanging a picture and he hit his thumb with the hammer," said Greg.

"Well, Greg dearie, that's not so terrible," his

46

mother soothed. "You shouldn't cry over a little thing like that. Why didn't you just laugh?"

"I did," sobbed Greg.

107. Headline in the *Nogales International* of Arizona: CHILDBIRTH IS BIG STEP TO PARENTHOOD.

108. These days, for many women, natural childbirth is a very important set of techniques. It involves no use of painkilling drugs, and the teaching of physical and mental techniques for reducing pain and heightening joyful awareness. Often the husband of the expectant mother is an important companion and participant in the process.

However, in late 1992 I saw a headline in *USA Today*: DOLPHINS DO DELIVERY. It seems that eight British expectant mothers headed for Eilat, Israel's Red Sea resort, to try the latest natural childbirth technique—using dolphins as midwives. Dolphins, as you may know, are aquatic mammals who navigate by the gentle means of echolocation (sound waves that echo back) and who are exceptionally friendly toward humans.

The eight women spent a part of every day swimming, with dolphins in attendance. Says trainer Sophie Schwer of Eilat's Dolphin Reef: "With dolphins the baby [is] . . . more calm and open."

Question: Could this become a new source of revenue for zoos and aquariums?

109. A very blond mother is married to a Chinese man. Their baby was born early—while the husband was away on business.

The nurse-midwife who assisted with the birth exclaimed after the baby was born, "Why, this baby is Chinese!"

"What do you expect?" replied the mother. "One baby in four is Chinese."

These days, self-esteem is considered very important to a person's well-being. And it long has been. Remember, when Jesus was asked by a teacher of the Law, "Which commandment is the most important of all?" he did not mention any of the so-called Ten Commandments. What he replied was, "Hear, O Israel; The Lord our God is one Lord," and "Thou shalt love thy neighbor *as thyself*" [emphasis added].

110. A set of numerical facts can help you and your children feel important. You had two parents. Each of your parents had two parents, and they had a total of four parents. Before that, you had eight great-grandparents, sixteen great-great-grandparents, 32 great-great-great-grandparents. If you figure an average of 25 years between generations, only 500 years ago there were 1,048,576 people on Earth involved in the production of you!

111. A man said to a friend: "My wife is suing my parents for giving birth to me."

112. Mrs. Crayshaw heard a crash in the kitchen. She shouted, "More dishes, Mike?"

"No," replied Mike, "fewer dishes."

Yes, it can be tough to be a parent, but remember that there can be problems about being a child.

113. A fifth-grade class was assigned to write an essay on parents. One girl's essay started: "The trouble with parents is that when we get them they are so old it is very hard to change their habits."

114. A stout schoolteacher was discussing with her class birds and their habits. She said, "At home I have a canary, and it can do something that I can't do. Can any of you tell what that thing is?"

Little Roger raised his hand.

"Yes, Roger?" said the teacher.

"The canary can take a bath in a saucer," said Roger.

115. This exchange took place at the supper table:
Kid: "I want some more pie!"
Parent: "What do you say?"
Kid: "Now!"

116. Young Oscar was a lively and curious kid. He was looking at the full moon and asked, "Dad, is God in the moon?"

"God is everywhere," Dad explained.

"Is he in my tummy?" asked Oscar.

"Well," Dad replied, "I suppose he is."

"O.K.!" declared Oscar. "God wants a banana."

117. A lonely child, wanting companions, once said to his mother, "I wish I were two little puppies so that I could play together."

Young children can sometimes make quite intelligent mistakes in language. Here are three examples from my own grandchildren.

118. Molly's mother to her then 4½-year-old daughter who was leaving the room: "What are you going to do, Molly?"

Molly: "Urinate."

Sister Anna, 2½ years old: "I'm an ate, too."

119. The same Molly, when 5½, was reporting on a friend's visit to New York City. "They saw something very exciting," said Molly.

"What was that?" asked her parents.

"The Ampark Stapledy," said Molly.

It took quite a while, after Molly described the Ampark Stapledy, to figure out that what she was referring to was the Empire State Building.

120. Yet another grandchild, Laura, at age 4½, was heard by her parents loudly chewing ice. They'd told Laura before that such chewing might be bad for her teeth. Laura's mother said, "What are you doing, chewing ice again?"

"No," replied Laura. "I'm making water."

121. A young husband came home from work to find his wife crying.

Wife: "I've had an awful day."

Husband: "I'm sorry, dear. What happened? Tell me."

Wife: "Baby cut his first tooth and took his first step—"

Husband (interrupting): "But that's wonderful!"

Wife: "Then Baby fell down and cut his lip on his tooth and said his first word."

122. A young couple had their first baby. When it was one year old, it hadn't said a word; one and a half years old, still not a word. The parents took the baby to a pediatrician, who said, "Everything's perfectly normal. Just be patient."

And so it went until the child's 25th month. They

were all having breakfast and the kid turned to his mother and said, "This oatmeal is too damn lumpy!"

The parents were amazed, and so they said, "Why haven't you talked before?"

The kid replied, "Up till now, things have gone very well."

123. Young Blake visited a neighbor's house. "Can I see your trap?"

"What trap? I don't know what you mean." said the neighbor.

Blake replied, "The one my dad says you can't keep shut."

124. Eleven-year-old Josh was talking to his parents about an overactive friend. He said, "Billy is a kind of sonic boom with dirt all over it."

(In case you don't know, a sonic boom is a violent shock wave produced by an object moving through the air faster than the speed of sound—like a jetliner.)

125. As Dad came home from work and opened the door, his nine-year-old daughter, standing beside her mother, said, "A motion has just been made and seconded that we go out for dinner."

Sometimes youngsters observe life's situations and

come up with very intelligent questions—or even answers or solutions.

126. As young Jesse and his mother were riding the department store escalator down, the boy asked, "Mom, what happens when the basement gets full of steps?"

127. At another department store, a small boy was standing at the foot of the down escalator, looking intently at the moving handrail. The store manager, walking by, stopped and asked, "Is there something wrong, sonny?"

"Nope," replied the boy. "I'm just waiting for my bubble gum to come back."

128. Albert Einstein enjoyed children. One day one of Einstein's young friends proudly presented his 18-month-old son to the scientist. When the child looked up into the old man's face, he promptly began to howl. Einstein patted him on the head and said fondly to the father, "He's the first person in years who's told me what he really thinks of me."

129. A Philadelphia family enjoyed collecting postcard photographs of classic works of art. The young children enjoyed looking at them. One day their parents suggested that they all visit the famous Philadelphia Museum of Art. They were enthusiastic, and so the visit took place.

As the family walked around the rooms full of classic paintings, the parents heard the kids saying, over and over, "We already have that," "We already have that."

130. Little Millie had gone to bed, and her father was downstairs reading the paper. A terrible thunderstorm came up, with lightning and fierce noises. Milly shouted down to her father, "Daddy, I'm scared! Come up and help me."

Milly's father, engrossed in the paper, shouted back, "Don't worry, Milly. You'll be all right. You know God loves you!"

"I know God loves me," cried Milly, "but I need something with skin on."

A grandparent can often teach children—indirectly, perhaps—to say thank-you for presents.

131. Mrs. Gehrig used to give generous Christmas presents to her several grandchildren, but the kids never sent thank-you notes, despite the urging of their father and mother. But then one year things changed. Grandma sent a generous Christmas check to each grandchild. The very next day, each child came over in person to thank her. She was telling this to a friend of hers, who said, "How wonderful! What do you think caused them to become so polite?"

"Well," said Grandma, "it was easy. This year I didn't sign the checks."

We'll close this chapter with four items about family relationships not directly involving children.

132. An insurance executive friend of mine, Frank Stull, who is a twinkly-wise humorous man, states this truth: "Behind every successful man there stands a surprised mother-in-law."

133. A famous stalwart, honest Quaker, Shippen Lewis, who died about fifty years ago at an advanced age, once said, "Of all my wife's relations, I like myself the best."

134. Joseph Cook (1838–1901), the great American lecturer, neatly stated the problems of life: "Striving twenties, thriving thirties, fiery forties, faithful fifties, sober sixties, solemn seventies, aching eighties, the sod, God!"

135. An anonymous saying from a wise Asian has it that a young man said to a very old man, "What is your greatest burden as you grow old?"

The ancient one replied, "My greatest burden is that I have nothing to carry." Modern studies do not confirm this view. See my book *Older and Wiser—*

Wit, Wisdom, and Spirited Advice from the Older Generation, Walker Publishing Company, 1986. To order, call 1-800-289-2553.)

5.

Problems of Life

Perhaps every chapter of this book could be, in some sense, titled "Problems of Life." But, as we've suggested, humor and problems are closely interrelated.

136. An angry man finally exploded: "I hate everybody regardless of race, gender, creed, or place of national origin!"

And perhaps there can be a bit of anger (and sense of perspective) in young females.

137. A fifth-grade girl started her homework essay on men thus: "Men are what women marry. They drink and smoke and swear, but don't go to church. They are more logical than women and also more zoological. Both men and women sprung from monkeys, but the women sprung further than the men." (See story number 576 for Mark Twain's view on this subject.)

Then there are problems of confinement and coverage.

138. According to the *Los Angeles Times*, San Diego County sometimes has difficulty getting people to accept jury duty. One man replied to his summons: "I would be most happy to serve, but first you will have to make arrangements for my release from jail."

139. A counselor working in a prison asked an inmate why he was incarcerated. The reply: "Someone yelled, 'Stop, thief!'—and, like a fool, I stopped."

140. One winter, two New York impoverished gentlemen were lying on a park bench under piles of newspaper to keep them warm. Said one to the other: "This is the time of year when you begin to appreciate the *Times*'s fuller coverage."

141. An anonymous rhymster tells us:
    The rain falls on the just
    And on the unjust fella,
    But mostly on the just
    Because the unjust
    Has the just's umbrella.

And another kind of coverage.

142. When I asked my cousin to help me with some paperwork, he regretfully refused, saying, "I have such a pile of things to do on my desk that sometimes when I get to the bottom, it's turned to compost."

Now back to another kind of confinement.

143. A farmer was having trouble managing the birth of a calf. He saw a man (who happened to be a city drunk) wandering down the lane beside his farm.

"Hey, stranger!" called the farmer. "How about giving me a hand?"

The drunk obliged, and in half an hour the calf was delivered. The drunk, exhausted, sat down and then looked the calf in the face and said, "Shay, don't you *ever* get in there again!"

Some people feel confined by living in a small town—and some don't.

144. When asked where he lived, Mr. Pinker replied, "Tuckahoe, New Jersey."

"Where's that? I've never heard of it," said the inquirer.

"Never heard of it?" exclaimed Mr. Pinker. "Why, you can go *anywhere* from Tuckahoe!"

Have you ever felt confined on an airplane? Well, an elderly friend of mine told this story.

145. It was on one of the early nonstop flights on a four-motored, propeller-driven plane from New York to Los Angeles. About an hour out of New York, one of the motors failed. Said the pilot over the intercom, "Ladies and gentlemen, we have lost one of our motors, but don't worry, this plane can fly on three engines. The only problem is that we'll be half an hour late arriving in L.A."

An hour later, a second motor failed. Said the pilot, "Ladies and gentlemen, we've lost a second engine. But don't worry. This plane can fly on two engines."

However, forty-five minutes later, a third engine failed. Said the pilot, "Ladies and gentlemen, this is strange, but we've lost a third engine. However, not to worry. The plane can fly on one engine. I regret, though, that we'll be three hours late getting into L.A."

At this point a frustrated passenger called out, "My God, if we lose our fourth engine, we'll never come down!"

Now let's go on to other problems of life. We'll look at them in miscellaneous order, since that's the way life usually presents them.

One problem is that we human beings are so preoccupied with what has happened before, and what will happen, that we never enjoy *now*!

146. Joel Goodman, head of *The Humor Project* in Saratoga Springs, New York, and editor of *Laughing Matters*, was interviewing comedian Sid Caesar in 1992. Caesar said this in the interview: "There are the Nows, Was's, and Gonna-Be's. A Now is the most precious thing you can have, because a Now goes by with the speed of light. Let's say you're having a beautiful Now that you want to hold on to forever. No matter how much you want to hold on to it, it's going to be a Was. A lot of people get stuck in and can't let go of the Was's. Those Was's get heavy, and they start to decay into Shoulda-Couldas. And they never have time for the new Now."

A "Now" and a "Gonna Be" is the environment, a problem.

147. A middle-aged man said to his objecting wife, "It's not called burping anymore. It's called oxygen recycling and it's good for the planet."

148. At a supermodern supermarket, the checkout people are trained to ask each customer: "Do you want to endanger the environment with plastic or would you rather destroy a tree by using a paper bag?"

How about people's bad opinion of themselves or others?

149. Said W. S. Gilbert (1836–1911) of the famous Gilbert and Sullivan operettas, "You've no idea what a poor opinion I have of myself, and how little I deserve it."

150. After many sessions, a psychiatrist said to one of his patients, "Maybe you don't have a complex—maybe you *are* inferior."

151. Some Welshmen, rather under the influence, were traveling home from Paddington train station in London. As they proceeded, they shouted, "Hurrah for Wales!" Finally a rather dour-looking Englishman couldn't take it any longer. He turned toward the Welshmen and retorted, "Hurrah for hell!"

"Fair enough," replied a Welshman. "Every man for his own country!"

152. Georg Christoph Lichtenberg (1742–1799) was a German physicist and satirist, a specialist in electricity. He also had very large ears. Once a friend of Lichtenberg's made fun of him for this. The physicist replied with a laugh, "Well, it's remarkable. With my ears and your brain, we'd make a perfectly splendid jackass."

153. According to Milton Segal of Warner Brothers, a man was heard to say, "I'm a walking economy. My hairline's in recession, my waist is a victim of inflation, and together they're putting me into a deep depression."

154. A countryman went to Dublin and was driving the wrong way on a one-way street. A policeman stopped him and said, "Where do you think you are going?"

The countryman replied, "I'm not sure, but I reckon I'm late. Everybody appears to be going home."

155. While we're on the subject of Dublin, Ireland, and the questionable behavior there, it will be illuminating to read this letter that appeared in the *Irish Times*:

Sir,

Teagasc runs the College of Horticulture in the ICA buildings at Termonfeckin, Co Louth. This is a residential third-level institution with an important role to play in the development of a skilled pool of horticulturalists for the Irish industry.

I know, therefore, that many will want to join me in congratulating the college on its decision to suspend three students last month. Two girls were found drinking tea in a boy's room at 9:30 P.M. These students may be as young as 18 or 19 years of age and it is vital that they be taught a severe lesson now if we are to have mature and responsible horticulturalists for the 90s and the next century.

Such social mixing must be avoided at all costs and this, indeed, was a blatant breach of regulations which absolutely forbid such fraternisation. Happily, there are now regular patrols of the boys' corridors to ensure that is not repeated.

> Yours, etc.,
> Diarmuid Barry,
> Annamore,
> 30 Sydney Avenue
> Blackrock, Co Dublin.

Now let's consider some bad behavior in another English-speaking country that is not the U.S.A.

156. In a suburb of Sydney, Australia, there was a rash of vandalism on the streets. On one street, some 30 parked cars had their tires punctured during the night by what appeared to be an ice pick.

The residents of the street were determined to catch and punish the vandal, so they set up a hidden video and let it run all night. The next morning they eagerly watched the tape, and the culprit was recognized.

It was a cattle dog that was sinking its teeth into tires.

Punishment? The dog was banished to the country.

157. A man had bought a farm on the Canadian border of North Dakota. He had lived there for many years when an official in uniform came to his house and said, "Sir, I have some news for you. It may be upsetting."

The man looked concerned. "Well, tell me," he said, "what is the news?"

The official explained, "When the border between Canada and the United States was established years ago, a mistake was made. Actually, sir, the U.S.-Canadian border is on the south side of your property, not the north."

The man smiled and said, "Why, I'm delighted!"

The official was surprised. "Why are you so pleased?" he asked.

He replied, "Now I'll never have to live through another North Dakota winter."

In our lives, many of us have problems with *things*—objects, etc.

158. In a small weekly paper in South Carolina this ad appeared: "FOR SALE—VCR. LIKE NEW. NEVER FIGURED OUT."

Smoking has become a very *real* problem of life.

159. This poster was seen in a public building: "If you must smoke, DO NOT EXHALE."

160. What things to keep, what things to throw away? That's a question we often ask ourselves, and there seems to be a law of behavior concerning it: The average time between throwing something away and needing it badly is about ten days.

And sometimes "things" are more in the mind and wit than in actual existence.

161. Mr. Evans was walking past a retirement home in Seattle. As he went by, he noticed an elderly gentleman reclining in a chair, holding a fishing rod with the line out on the lawn. Said Mr. Evans, "Caught anything yet?"

Replied the oldster, "You're the first."

Will the time come when we run completely out of things?

162. A wise man connected with the *Times* of Reading, Pennsylvania, asked his readers: "Who's going to do all the work in this world when the trend toward extended education meets the trend toward early retirement?"

163. One of the problems with lots of *things* is that they are made for right-handed people. And yet some 10% of people are left-handed, and they suffer from the world's bias in favor of the right hand. Fossil evidence shows that this has been the case for over a million years.

There is an organization whose headquarters are in Topeka, Kansas. Their title is Lefthanders International. They pointed out that during the 1992 presidential election campaign, when it was a three-way race, all three candidates, George Bush, Bill Clinton, and Ross Perot, were lefties. (So were Presidents Gerald Ford, Harry Truman, and James Garfield. Ronald Reagan was a southpaw who was forced to switch sides.)

Some other famous lefties are Leonardo da Vinci (1452–1519), Michelangelo Buonarroti (1475–1564), Babe Ruth (1895–1948) . . . and we could go on.

While we are thinking about hands, handedness, and the problems of life, let's consider some wise and humorous words on the subject.

164. A columnist named Simeon Stylites, whose name was adopted from that of the Syrian hermit (390?–459?) who lived for over thirty-five years on a small platform atop a large pillar, wrote: "There are four things one can do with his hands: (1) wring them in despair; (2) fold them in apathy; (3) put them in his pocket for safekeeping; *or* (4) lay them on a job that needs doing."

We'll close this chapter in a way that leads nicely into the next chapter: "Human Behavior." It is another way of saying what we should do with our hands as well as our energy and ideas.

165. Henry Joel Cadbury (1883–1974) was Professor of Divinity at Harvard, Chairman of the American Friends Service Committee (Quakers), and one of the translators of the Revised Standard Version of the New Testament. He certainly was one to lay his hands on a job worth doing. Once in a Friends Meeting for Worship, he rose and said:

"There are two kinds of Friends in our Society, and two kinds of people in the world: the *therefore* people and the *however* people. *Therefore* people say, 'We need to deal with the problem of hunger in poor countries and in our own country. *Therefore* . . .' and they go on to say what actions they will undertake. *However* people make the same beginning statement but follow it with, '*However* . . .' and they explain why nothing can be done.

"Try it for yourself after each of these statements: 'We must improve race relations in the city of Boston . . .'; 'This morning I decided to volunteer at least two hours a week in our neighborhood nursing home . . .'; 'I am amazed at the amount of litter dropped in our city parks . . .'

"We need fewer *however* people in the world and among Quakers. We need more *therefore* people."

Therefore, not however, turn now to "Manners—
Good, Bad, and Peculiar; and Even Artistic."

6.

Manners—Good, Bad, and Peculiar; and Even Artistic

Who knows whether human manners are part of the problems of life or part of their solution?

166. The great French military commander of World War I, Marshal Ferdinand Foch (1851–1929), not only knew his armies (in 1918 he commanded the British, French, and U.S. Armies); he also knew about manners. When an American complained to him about the insincere politeness of the French, saying, "There is nothing in it but wind," Foch replied, "There's nothing but wind in a tire, but it makes riding in a car very smooth and pleasant."

Now here are some examples of human manners. My readers will have to judge whether they are like wind in a tire.

167. Lady Astor (1879–1964) was born in Virginia as Nancy Langhorne. She was the first woman member of British Parliament (1919–1945) and the epitome of British aristocracy. Once, during a party she held at her ornate residence on the Thames, Lady Astor learned that Turner Catledge, then an editor of the *New York Times*, was present and was from Mississippi. She shouted, "Where is that southern white trash?" Then she went over to Catledge and said, "Shake! I'm southern white trash, too."

168. A rich lady gave a little boy two cents. When the boy was silent, she said, "What does a gentleman say when he is given two pennies?"

The boy replied, "I'm too much of a gentleman to tell you."

169. Miss Steinbright was standing in front of her third-grade class. For some reason she said to the students, "Will anyone who thinks he or she is stupid please stand up."

There was a brief silence and then Jenny stood. Miss Steinbright was surprised. She said, "Why, Jenny, you're not stupid, are you?"

"No, Teacher," replied Jenny, "but I couldn't leave you standing up there alone."

170. The great French writer François-Marie Arouet de Voltaire (1694–1778) was talking with a friend, who said about a mutual acquaintance, "It's good of you to say such pleasant things of him when he says such spiteful ones of you."

"Perhaps," replied Voltaire, "we are both mistaken."

171. George Santayana (1863–1952) was born in Spain but taught at Harvard for many years. He often received gifts of books from various authors. He told a friend, "It is part of prudence to thank an author for his book before reading it, so as to avoid the necessity of lying about it afterward."

Now let's go on to some stories about various works of art—or the artists.

172. *The Spectator*, a well-known publication in England, ran this review: "A book with a message not even a pigeon would carry."

173. A theater review of a play: "The big trouble was that the seats faced the stage."

174. Julie Salamon of *The Wall Street Journal* made this comment about a film: "Most of the actors came into this project anonymously, and that's how they'll leave it—if they're lucky."

175. George S. Kaufman (1889–1961), the American playwright, said, "When a play receives mixed reviews, it means it's good and rotten."

Perhaps we should move briefly into the field of music and "manners"—or maybe the manners of musicians.

176. George Jean Nathan (1882–1958), the American editor and drama critic, wrote erudite and cynical reviews. Thus, not everyone liked him, including the songwriter Cole Porter (1893–1964). Once Porter wrote: "Critic George Jean Nathan is so tone-deaf that he only recognizes 'The Star Spangled Banner' because people stand up when it's played."

177. A famous conductor, Sir Malcolm Sargent, was asked, "What do you have to know to play the cymbals?"

"Nothing," replied Sargent, "except when."

178. And here's a story about the opposite aspect of playing. Artur Schnabel (1882–1951) said, "The notes I handle no better than many pianists. But pauses between the notes—ah, that is where the art resides!"

179. Oscar Levant (1906–1972) was brilliantly playing George Gershwin's Piano Concerto in F. It was in a college auditorium, and a telephone began ringing loudly in a nearby office. After a time, the audience began squirming. Then Levant looked at the audience and, without interrupting his playing, said loudly, "If that's for me, tell them I'm busy."

And some other aspects of manners:

Manners and Food

180. Mrs. Dalgiri was standing in the checkout line of a supermarket. Suddenly she was pushed aside by another woman who shouted, "Checker, ring up my ten cans of cat food, quick!" Then she turned to Mrs. Dalgiri and said, "I hope you don't mind waiting."

"Oh, no," replied Mrs. Dalgiri with a sweet smile, "not if you're that hungry."

181. One night young Kate pushed back her chair from the dinner table and explained, "I'm full. I wanna leave!"

Her grandfather, speaking so quickly that her grandmother could not get in a reprimand, said, "What you mean, Kate, is 'My Plimsoll line is underwater.'"

"Oh, excuse me," said Kate. "But what does that mean?"

Granddad explained that it is a line on a boat that

shows when full cargo has been loaded. And from that night on, when Kate and her siblings wanted to leave, they said, "My Plimsoll line is underwater," and the grandmother would respond with a smile, "You are excused from the table."

182. Hardworking, expert cook Mrs. Webster always served a delicious meal to her family of six. But one evening she smilingly set before each person a plate of straw.

"Hey!" said an amazed son. "What goes on here?"

"Well," replied Mrs. Webster, "I didn't think you'd notice. You never mention the food."

From that time on, the housewife—to use an old-fashioned term—got plenty of praise for her cooking.

Perhaps this rhyme should be posted, large-print, in your living room and/or drawing room!

183. Maurice Sendak, author and illustrator of *Where the Wild Things Are* and other children's books, gets many fan letters from young readers. He says that one of his favorites was a cute drawing sent on by a small boy's mother. Sendak says, "I loved it, and I drew a picture of a Wild Thing on a postcard and sent it to the boy. The boy's mother wrote back: 'Jim loved your card so much, he ate it.'

"The little boy," Sendak continues, "didn't care that it was an original drawing. He saw it, he loved it, he ate it. That was one of the highest compliments I've ever received."

184. Clare Boothe Luce (1903–1987), a remarkable woman, wrote *The Women* and was, among other things, wife of Henry Robinson Luce, founder of *Time* magazine, U. S. representative from Connecticut, and ambassador to Italy. She attended a fashionable dinner party and was seated next to David Burpee, chairman of Burpee's Seed Company. As they talked, Burpee realized that Clare Luce had forgotten his name, so to put her at ease, he whispered, "I'm Burpee."

Luce looked at him in a puzzled way and then smiled and patted his hand. "That's all right," she said, "I get that way sometimes myself."

Manners and "breeding"

185. Mrs. W. Newton Gilpin, a "veddy" aristocratic Lady, was shopping for a dog. She went to a kennel owner and, after looking around, said, "I want a dog of which I can be proud. Does this one have a good pedigree?"

"Mrs. Gilpin," said the kennel owner, "if he could talk, he wouldn't speak to either of us."

186. Mrs. Palmer and Mrs. Palmer were introduced to each other at a very fancy tea. Mrs. Palmer (#1) was a society lady from New York City, and she was trying to find out the background of the other Mrs. Palmer (#2).

Finally Mrs. Palmer (#2) said, "I'm a member of the Palmer family from Mauchchunk, Pennsylvania."

Mrs. Palmer (#1) stuck her nose in the air and said, "In New York we think that breeding is everything."

Mrs. Palmer (#2) replied, "In Mauchchunk we think it's lots of fun, but it isn't everything."

187. Speaking of breeding, one can't be too careful—even in libraries. A Victorian woman, Lady Gough, who flourished in the late 18th century, wrote a very properly British *Lady Gough's Book of Etiquette*. Among her strict pronouncements was the forbidding of placing books written by male authors next to books written by female "authoresses." However, married authors like Robert Browning and Elizabeth Barrett Browning could be placed together without impropriety.

Manners and Truth

What is "the truth"? Perhaps good manners help to obscure it, or perhaps, subtly, to reveal it.

188. A pompous and arrogant Mrs. J. Pinfield Girard was visiting the antique shop of Mr. Joseph Alcorn. She was obviously just passing the time, making Mr. Alcorn drag out old pieces and then commenting on their high prices and poor quality. After about an hour, she looked at her watch and said, "Mr. Alcorn, I must go. I suppose that you think that I'm a nuisance, just pretending that I know what I'm talking about."

Mr. Alcorn bowed graciously. "If you say so, my dear lady," he said. "In my shop, the customer is always right."

189. A Maine lobsterman, James Stockton, made good income hauling "trippers" in his fishing boat. He was known far and wide for the yarns he spun. One day, a newcomer, an ample widow still wearing her city clothes and sporting her city manners, raised her voice against the wind and shrilled, "Captain, they tell me you're the biggest liar on the Maine coast."

Captain Stockton swept off his battered straw hat, bowed in as courtly a gesture as the roll of the sea would permit, and said, "Madame, you are the most beautiful woman I ever saw in my life."

Supermiscellaneous

190. A careful observer of human habits stated: "When a man opens the door of his car for his wife, you can be sure that either the car or the wife is new."

191. A "weighty" Quaker, William Bacon Evans (1875–1964), was always welcome at all Friends Meetings because of his terse religious utterances and vast fund of wit. Once, when he was playing soccer for Haverford College against Columbia University, he and a Columbia player crashed into each other as they went for the ball. "Jesus Christ!" exclaimed the opponent. "No," said Evans, "just one of his humble servants," and he dribbled the ball away with vigor and, it is said, scored a goal.

192. Conrad Hilton, the hotel man, had a well-disciplined wit. Once he was on the Johnny Carson show, and he was asked if he had a message for the American people. He looked straight into the camera and said, slowly and distinctly to about 30 million listeners, "Please put the shower curtain inside the tub."

On what better (and wetter) note could we now turn to the next chapter? It's titled "Human Behavior—So What Else Isn't?"

7.

Human Behavior—So What Else Isn't?

Undoubtedly a problem of human behavior is temptation. Of course, temptation is not evil; only actions can be evil.

193. But Oscar Wilde thought differently. He said, "The only way to get rid of temptation is to yield to it."

194. But sometimes it's not possible to yield to temptation. For example, a small-town newspaper was running a competition to discover the most high-principled, sober, well-behaved local citizen. Among the entries came one that read:

"I don't smoke, touch intoxicants, or gamble. I am faithful to my wife and never look at another woman. I am hardworking, quiet, and obedient. I never go to the movies or the theater, and I go to bed early every night and rise with the dawn. I attend chapel regularly every Sunday without fail.

"I've been like this for the past three years. But just wait until next spring, when they let me out of here!"

195. A business friend and cousin of mine—who has reached the age of eighty-one—says of temptation: "All the things we like to do are illegal, immoral, or fattening."

196. George Moore (1852–1933), the Irish-born English author of *A Modern Lover*, *A Mummer's Wife*, and *Esther Waters*, was famous in London as a great lover. On his eightieth birthday, he was asked how he continued to enjoy such excellent health. He replied: "It's because I never smoked, or drank, or touched a girl—until I was eleven years old."

197. Some creatures don't sleep, but they may have a distorted sense of their own importance. There was a rooster who thought that the sun rose every morning just to hear him crow.

I guess roosters don't ask many questions. Their own individual importance is obvious to them. But it's not that way with most great people.

198. Rudyard Kipling (1865–1936) examined life vigorously and carefully. He wrote:

> I had six honest serving men
> They taught me all I knew;
> Their names were Where and
>   What and When
> And Why and How and Who.

199. Another seeker after knowledge—perhaps more profound, less nationalistic and patriotic than Kipling—was Niels Bohr (1885–1962), the great Danish physicist who won the Nobel prize for his work on atomic structure and helped to create the atom bomb. He frequently told his students: "Every sentence I utter must be understood, not as an affirmative, but as a question." Albert Einstein (1875–1955) said, "Bohr is one of the most amiable colleagues I have ever met. He utters opinions like one perpetually groping, and never like one who believes himself to be in possession of definite truth."

200. But more about Einstein, and a less modest man—Sir Arthur Stanley Eddington (1882–1944), who taught at Cambridge University and directed an observatory there. Eddington promoted Einstein's theory of relativity. Once he was asked, "Is it true, Professor, that you are one of the three people in the world who understand Einstein's theory of relativity?"

Eddington hesitated.

"I'm sorry," said his interviewer. "I should have realized a man of your modesty would find that question embarrassing."

"Not at all," Eddington replied. "I was just trying to think who the third might be."

Was Eddington modest? I don't know, but some old people aren't—well, not *very*.

201. Josiah Pepper was celebrating his 100th birthday in a nursing home. Reaching age 100 is quite an event, so a local TV reporter interviewed Mr. Pepper.

Reporter: "Are you able to get out and walk much?"

Pepper: "Well, I certainly walk better today than I did a hundred years ago."

202. Upon turning 95, George Burns said, "I look better, feel better, make love better, and I'll tell you something else—I never lied better."

203. Yes, George Burns is old and happy, and apparently he has no wish to be young again. Perhaps he would agree with Samuel Butler (1612–1680), the great English poet and satirist. In one of his mellower moments he wrote:

"Youth is like spring, an overpraised season more remarkable for biting winds than genial breezes. Autumn is the mellower season, and what we lose in flowers, we more than gain in fruits."

204. And who was it who said, "America would have been a better place if Plymouth Rock had landed on the Pilgrims instead of the other way round"?

An aspect of human behavior is cynicism. It comes with all ages.

205. The humorist Dorothy Parker (1893–1967) wrote:

Three are the things I shall have till I die:
Laughter, and hope—and a sock in the eye.

206. Many writers sought the criticism of the great American poet Carl Sandburg (1878–1967). Once a playwright asked him to attend a dress rehearsal of his play. Sandburg agreed, but he fell asleep during the performance. The playwright was angry. "Don't you know how much I needed your opinion?" he protested.

Sandburg replied, "Sleep *is* an opinion."

207. A friend told me about a small boy, Ezra, who usually was driven to school—in great haste—by his father. But one day his mother drove him. After a peaceful few minutes, Ezra asked, "Mom, where are all the bastards, damn fools, and S.O.B.s?"

"Oh," replied his mother, "they only come out when your father's driving."

208. But nobody's perfect, thank God! An interesting comment on "perfect" people was made by Cardinal Richard Cushing (1895–1970) of Boston. He said, "Saints are okay in Heaven, but they're hell on earth." (I had a religious, humorous aunt who said—often—"A martyr is someone who has to live with a saint.")

209. From 1949 to 1951, a cousin of mine, Comfort Cary Richardson, did relief work with the American Friends Service Committee (Quakers) in the Gaza Strip, a place of great conflict between Arabs and Jews. One of the qualities of Quakers is that they believe in (and pretty well practice) loving all people. But when someone asked Comfort's mother how her daughter was doing in Gaza, the reply was: "She's doing very well, but as for those Arabs—she *loathes* loving them."

210. Mark Twain enjoyed being naughty in many delightful ways. Once he wrote: "I think that the unbroken monotony of [my brother Henry's] goodness and truthfulness and obedience would have been a burden to [my mother] but for the relief and variety I furnished in the other direction."

This may explain why Twain, when asked where he would like to go when he died, replied, "Well, Heaven for the climate, hell for the company."

211. Walter Elias Disney (1901–1966) was about as famous as any American ever was or will be. But once a friend asked him how it feels to be a celebrity. He replied: "It feels good when it helps to get a good seat for a football game. But it never helped me make a good film or a good shot in a polo game, or command the obedience of my daughter.

"It doesn't even seem to keep the fleas off our dogs—and if being a celebrity won't give me an advantage over a couple of fleas, then I guess there can't be much in being a celebrity after all."

212. In his book *Deadline*, *New York Times* reporter James (Scottie) Reston wrote that "sometimes it takes a major surgical operation to get an idea into a Scotman's head," but another man had an even more vivid way of saying the same thing about all of us. He was Charles Franklin Kettering (1876–1958), the great American electrical engineer and inventor. He wrote: "You can send a message around the world in one fifth of a second, yet it may take years for it to get from the outside of man's head to the inside."

Perhaps hell is an interesting place. If you were a tourist, would you like to go there? Would you choose the smoking or the no-smoking section?

213. Probably the world's most famous volcano is Mount Vesuvius. In one eruption, 1631, 18,000 people were killed. Well, a bunch of tourists were looking over the ruin of Vesuvius, and one American said to another, "My God! It sure is deep and hot! Reminds you of hell, doesn't it?"

A local guide, hearing the comment, said quietly to another European beside him, "These Americans! They've been everywhere."

214. Certainly several people can look at the same thing and have different reactions. An archaeologist, a clergyman, and a cowboy were looking down into Grand Canyon. The archaeologist exclaimed, "What a wonder of science!" The clergyman said reverently, "One of the glories of God." The cowboy commented, "A helluva place to lose a cow."

215. And there are those who are exposed to tourists. One of the greatest states to tour in is Maine—scenery, great seafood, and accents. One tourist was talking to a Mainer and observed, "There certainly are a lot of peculiar people around here."

"Ayuh," replied the local, "but they all leave after the tourist season."

216. An American tourist was looking at a magnificent cathedral in Paris. He was not very well informed and had left his guidebook in the hotel, so he asked a Frenchman, "What is that wonderful building?"

The Frenchman replied, "That, monsieur, is Notre Dame."

"You've got to be kidding!" exclaimed the American, in a response that the Frenchman probably didn't understand. "Why, when I was in college, I *played* Notre Dame."

217. Yet another tourist, this one from Ireland, was Oscar Wilde (1854–1900). He was being given a tour of Niagara Falls. When the guide had given him all the amazing statistics, he turned to Wilde and said, "So what do you think?"

Wilde replied, " 'Twould be more impressive if it flowed the other way."

218. (The English essayist) Charles Lamb (1775–1834) was taking a lady tourist on a buggy ride in the beautiful countryside. On the way, they crossed a brook in which some youngsters were swimming—"skinny-dipping." The lady exclaimed, "Mr. Lamb, don't you think it's terrible! Those boys are swimming naked."

Replied Charles Lamb, "Oh, *I* hadn't noticed whether they were boys or girls."

219. Yet another tourist was visiting Texas. He decided to spend a day fishing. So he stopped at a small, not very elegant bait shop and asked a really lanky, white-bearded native Texan for 50 cents worth of worms. As the Texan dug into his great pile of worms, the tourist wondered whether he was going to have enough bait. He asked, "How many worms do I get for fifty cents?"

"Don't worry, son," the Texan replied. "I'll do right by you! Life's too short to be countin' worms."

And now a few miscellaneous bits and pieces about human—and subhuman—behavior.

220. Perseverance is very important to success. How else would two snails have made it to the ark?

221. How do you define a "split second"?—something snails don't worry about. A friend of mine says it's the moment between reading the freeway sign and realizing you've missed the off ramp.

222. Laurence J. Peter (1919–1990), the inventor of the Peter Principle, said, "A pessimist is a man who looks both ways before crossing a one-way street."

223. And another bit about transportation—and progress? Someone told me that his great-grandfather rode a horse but wouldn't go near a train. However, his grandfather loved trains but was scared of automobiles. Then his father happily drove a car but feared flying. Whereas the teller of this history of progress (??) loves to fly but doesn't dare to ride a horse.

224. As for fear, perhaps one could not say truthfully that Calvin Coolidge, President of the United States from 1923 to 1929, was afraid. However, he did state: "I have never been hurt by anything I didn't say."

225. Yes, Coolidge was a man of few words. Here's a five-point program for good human relations.

1. *I am proud of you*—five most important words.
2. *What is your opinion?*—four most important words.
3. *If you please*—three most important words.
4. *Thank you*—two most important words.
5. *I*—one *least* important word.

226. I'm not sure that this story can be verified. It's about Sir Noel Coward (1899–1973), the great British playwright, actor, and composer. It is said that he loved to play practical jokes. Once, it is said, he sent identical anonymous notes to twenty prominent Londoners: "All is discovered. Escape while you can." All twenty left town by morning.

227. Perhaps many more would have fled had they been required to recite a modern version of our Pledge of Allegiance. It goes: "I pledge allegiance to the flag of the United States of America and to the Republic for which it stands, one nation, under electronic surveillance, with mandatory urine testing and polygraphs for all."

I doubt whether the above amendment to the Pledge of Allegiance will make it into the mainstream, but it is at least an interesting "correction." Here's another totally different sort of correction.

228. The *Democrat and Chronicle* of Rochester, New York, published the following:
CORRECTION:
Erroneous information was inadvertently inserted into the biographical summary accompanying a story on Peter Keefe in Tuesday's *Democrat and Chronicle.* Keefe cannot simultaneously whistle, stand on his head, and drink beer.

For some, drinking is a popular form of human behavior, as the next two stories show.

229. In Wales, Evan Glendower was very fond of his "pint." Yet he was not a rich man and could ill afford stopping by the pub every evening on the way home from work.

One evening Evan made up his mind that he should mend his ways, and so, although greatly tempted, he walked right past the door of the pub and kept going for another half mile until he arrived at his own front door. Then he stopped, and a great smile appeared on his face. "Well done, Evan me man," he said. "Ye've made a splendid effort."

He turned around, continuing to talk to himself. "After a triumph like that, ye really deserve to go back to the pub and treat yourself to a pint!"

230. One evening William Wharton, a minor officer on a navy ship, staggered aboard the vessel, very drunk. His superior saw him and said, "Wharton, it's a pity you drink. If you were sober, you might have become a second officer like me. Think what drink has cost you!"

Wharton replied, "Nonsense! When I get a few drinks in me, I'm an admiral."

This seems like a cheerful note on which to go to the next chapter, "Doctors, Nurses, Medicine, and Health."

8.

Doctors, Nurses, Medicine, and Health

My son-in-law and his father, Herman "Hy" Weisberg, are doctors. Hy told about a patient of his. It has to do with that form of human behavior called *drinking* that we were just discussing in the previous chapter.

231. The patient was a man in his sixties. He was a smoker, a fat-eater, and, especially, a drinker. Dr. Weisberg warned him about the dangers of all these things, and said, "They may well cause you to die early."

The patient replied, "Doctor, you let me die, and I'll never speak to you again."

232. An opposite point of view was that of another patient of "Hy" Weisberg. The woman was of Puerto Rican origin, and she kept coming to Dr. Weisberg, who examined her thoroughly and kept finding, and saying, over and over, "Mrs. Donato, you're in good health."

One day Mrs. Donato retorted, "Doctor, one day I die of the good health."

One of the things that people hope is that their doctors and/or nurses will take careful care of them.

233. A competent, devotedly busy doctor was asked by a concerned friend of one of his patients whether the patient, Mrs. Springgarden, was being well taken care of. The doctor replied, "Well, I should tell you that I have so many pots burning right now, I'm almost overwhelmed, but *please* be assured that we're watching Mrs. Springgarden with a fine-toothed comb."

Doctors are, without doubt, very important to our health, but a lot of the major work is done by nurses.

234. When she was in a hospital, Dorothy Parker had her secretary visit to dictate some letters. She pressed the NURSE button and said, "That should assure us of at least forty-five minutes of undisturbed privacy."

However, there's another side to the nurse-arrival story.

235. On the way to the hospital, a nurse was driving very fast. She failed to heed the stoplight on the corner. A policeman caught up with her in the next block. Said he: "Doesn't that red light remind you of something?"

Replied the nurse: "Oh, yes, someone wants the bedpan."

And nurses have to deal with all sorts of human problems.

236. Mrs. Hall, a nurse, came to Mr. Gomez's hospital bed with a glass bottle for a urine specimen to be picked up later. Then came an attendant with the luncheon tray, which included a bottle of apple juice. Mr. Gomez poured the apple juice into the glass urine bottle.

Later, Mrs. Hall came in to pick up the specimen. She examined it and said, "Mr. Gomez, I don't think this looks quite right."

"I agree," said Mr. Gomez. "I'll just run it through again." With that, he drank the contents.

Mrs. Hall fainted.

237. We hear a good deal these days about sexual harassment. A few years ago, two nurses were looking at an old man in a wheelchair. One nurse said to the other, "Watch out for him. He's just had his wheels oiled."

238. Old age can be a concern, and many old people would pay quite a lot to live better and longer. Perhaps this explains a recent ad in the *Cleveland Plain Dealer*:

> At the Cleveland Clinic, Some of
> Our Surgeons
> Can Add Years to Your Life,
> Others Are Equally Expert at
> Reversing the Process.

Surgeons can be geniuses, but perhaps they're not perfect.

239. Mrs. Yarnall visited a surgeon to be examined for a painful condition. The surgeon looked her over and said, "You need an operation."

Mrs. Yarnall pondered and then said, "I'd like a second opinion."

"O.K.," replied the surgeon. "You don't need an operation."

240. Some doctors believe that it's important for the well-being of their patients that the doctor seem infallible. A medical friend of mine told a story about another doctor whose son had just graduated from medical school. He said to his son, "I want to give you some advice. Once you've made a diagnosis, don't let anybody change it."

Well, the young doctor's first patient was a large

woman complaining of abdominal pain. After examining her, he said, "Mrs. Shelby, your trouble is that you've got locked bowels."

The patient reacted, "But, Doctor, how could that be? I've got diarrhea."

Said the doctor, "I understand, Mrs. Shelby. The trouble is that they're locked in the open position."

My own able doctor often has humorous cartoons and drawings in his waiting room. However, he has none of these. (Perhaps he will have when he reads this book!)

241. In a dental office in California:

> OUR OFFICE POLICY IS TO DO OUR UTMOST TO SEE PATIENTS IN DISCOMFORT AS SOON AS POSSIBLE.

242. In a doctor's waiting room:

> DON'T ACT LIKE THIS: "I used to watch golf on TV, but I needed more exercise, so now I watch tennis."

243.

> IS YOUR BODY PRECIOUS? ITS TOTAL
> WORTH IS BETWEEN $5 AND $10.
> WHY? BECAUSE IT'S MOSTLY WATER
> PLUS A FEW CHEMICALS.

244.

> IS THIS A SHOPPING LIST?
>   CHEESE, COFFEE, SALT, DOUGHNUTS,
>   PORK CHOPS, CIGARETTES, BACON,
>   SUGAR, WHISKEY, GIN.
> NO, IT IS A SUICIDE LIST!

Some very famous writers have given vivid, specific descriptions of the human body and its condition.

245. Charles Dickens (1812–1870) had a bad cold and described it in a letter to a friend. "I am this moment deaf in the ears, hoarse in the throat, red in the nose, green in the gills, damp in the eyes, twitchy in the joints, and fractious in temper."

246. Joseph Addison (1672–1719), the British essayist, poet, and statesman, wrote in the June 12, 1711, edition of *The Spectator*: "I consider the Body as a System of Tubes and Glands, or to use a more Rustick phrase, a Bundle of Pipes and Strainers, fitted to one another after so wonderful a manner as to make it a proper Engine for the Soul to work with."

Maybe the body, thus defined, *is* worth more than $5–$10!

Is tippling the answer to our health problems? Probably not, because the problems and the elements involved in them are so complicated.

247. Northern Kentucky University, Highland Heights, Kentucky, has a newspaper *The Northerner*. The following announcement appeared in it recently:

Dr. Joseph Fondacaro, associate professor, Department of Physiology, College of Medicine, UC, will present a seminar in Natural Science 525 at noon. The topic is *Relationships between Bile Acids and Lipid Acids within the Small Intestine*. Everyone is encouraged to attend. Feel free to bring your lunch.

248. And perhaps words can be complicated, too. Mr. and Mrs. Washington, an elderly couple, married for many years, were watching a health program on TV. There was talk of high-risk groups and about AIDS. After the program, they were very concerned and made an appointment with their doctor.

"What's the problem?" asked the doctor.

"We're afraid we may be high risk for getting AIDS," said Mr. Washington.

"I shouldn't think so," said the doctor. "You're a loving, faithful couple and don't go running around."

"That's true," said Mrs. Washington. "But this TV program said that people most at risk are those who have annual sex."

Medical financial questions also can be a problem.

249. Many policyholders agree that Health insurance is like wearing a hospital gown. You only *think* you're fully covered.

250. Mr. Mallery had a bad heart. One day while he was at work, Mrs. Mallery received a telephone call saying that he had won $1,500,000 in the state lottery. She was concerned that the effect on him might be damaging, so she arranged for a psychologist friend to inform him and prepare him for the shock.

When they met, the psychologist said, "Suppose, Mr. Mallery, that you should win a lot of money. How would it affect you? What would you do?"

"Well," said Mr. Mallery quite happily, "if I won a lot of money, I admire you and your work so much that I'd give half of it to you."

The psychologist collapsed.

251. I have a good friend, Dr. Ramsey Thorp, who is

my ophthalmologist. He has a great many patients, so that it's sometimes difficult to get an appointment with him. He told me what to do if I wanted to see him quickly. "Just tell my secretary that you are an *aardvark*, and then give your name."

Well, I tried it, and it worked—and when I looked up *aardvark* in my dictionary I found that it is the very first real word listed, right after *aah*. I've wondered whether, if he doesn't particularly want to see a patient, he might say, "Tell my secretary you're a *zymosan*"—an insoluble largely polysaccharide fraction of yeast cell walls.

Mental and emotional problems are another type of medical complexity.

252. Fred Wilkinson had kidney problems. Every time he got excited, he wet his pants. It was very embarrassing, so he went to see his doctor, who gave him some pills. But they were of no help, so the doctor said, "Mr. Wilkinson, I suggest you see a psychiatrist."

He did so, and about a month later he had another visit with his doctor, who asked, "Well, how are you?"

Mr. Wilkinson replied, "I'm fine."

"Good," said the doctor.

"Yes, I'm fine," Mr. Wilkinson continued. "Of course, I still wet my pants, but it doesn't embarrass me anymore."

253. A woman patient had been going to a psychiatrist for three years. Finally, at the end of a visit, the doctor said, "It is my pleasure to pronounce you completely cured."

An unhappy expression came over the woman's face. "What's wrong?" asked the doctor. "I thought you'd be greatly pleased."

"That's what *you* thought," she said. "But look at it from my point of view. Three years ago, I was Joan of Arc. Now I'm nobody."

254. Another psychiatrist, after a long series of visits with a patient, sat back, looked sympathetically into the man's face, and said, "I've decided that you don't have an inferiority complex."

"Oh," said the patient. "Please explain."

The psychiatrist said, "It's not a complex. You really *are* inferior."

255. It is estimated that some 13 million Americans suffer from phobias. The word comes from the Greek *phobos*, meaning fear. I am one of the 13 million, and I suffer from *cyberphobia*. This is a fear of electronic devices—mechanical-electrical communication systems based on the science of cybernetics. To put it simply, I am afraid of word processors. I do all my typing on an old hand-powered Hermes portable typewriter, and I've written all of my 55 published books (including this one) by hand. (I have a wonderful typist who can decipher my scribbles and put my manuscripts in publishable form.)

What are some other phobias? Here are some other common phobias. Do you enjoy any of them as much as I enjoy my cyberphobia?

Phobia	*fear of*
acro	heights
agora	open spaces
claustro	enclosed areas
eosco	dawn
game	marriage
gephyro	bridges (crossing of)
hade	hell
harmato	error
homilo	sermons
neo	change
phasmo	ghosts
phobo	fear
tapho	being buried alive
triskaideka	thirteen
xeno	strangers
zelo	jealousy

So make up some of your own phobias (phobiae? phobiums?), and get some pleasure out of them.

The next chapter is titled "Business—Even the Military." The last story in *this* chapter leads nicely into the next.

256. A physician read a resolution at a local medical association meeting. After a pause, he said, "All in favor stick out your tongue and say, 'Ah.'"

If "Ah," turn to the next page.

9.

Business—Even the Military

It may seem strange to include the military in a chapter on business, but there are certainly business aspects to keeping the military going. The first 11 stories in this chapter relate to some of these aspects.

257. SPACEWALKING: Astronauts seem to most of us to have glamorous careers, and, one would think, highly paid ones. However, consider the case of *Apollo 16* crewman Charles Moss Duke, Jr. In his book *Moonwalker* he writes: "Astronauts were paid according to their rank. We did, however, get a little extra, as space flight was considered TDY, or temporary duty. The per diem for TDY at that time was $25. To claim credit, we had to fill out an itinerary. Mine read: Houston to Kennedy Space Center to moon, moon to Pacific Ocean, Pacific Ocean to Houston.

"The moon trip lasted 11 days, so that was $275 in extra money. However, as the government provided quarters and meals, that was deducted. I believe I made $1.25 for each day on the trip."

258. JOB ASSIGNMENT: A man was sent for training to Fort Bragg in Cumberland County, North Carolina. He had no idea what sort of job he would get, but the Army classification officer had no problem. The officer learned that the man had been a funeral director and embalmer in civilian life. Therefore, he was assigned to the Fort Bragg dead-letter office.

259. FAMILY INFLUENCE: A few years ago, the following form was enclosed with soldiers' allotment checks. "Class Q allotments are based upon the number of dependents up to a maximum of three, so if the birth of a child will mean your husband is entitled to more quarters allowance, notify him to take the necessary action."

260. ORGANIZATION OF DOCUMENTS: The Navy, like the other armed services, is constantly issuing orders, instructions, memorandums, revisions, etc., to clarify and simplify the already clarified and simplified. These efforts culminated in a recent instruction from the Navy. It read: "Classified material is considered lost when it cannot be found."

261. FEAR AND RESENTMENT OF AUTHORITY: A soldier telephoned the Army motor pool and asked, "What kinds of vehicles do you have for Army personnel to use?"

The soldier in charge of the motor pool replied, "For captains and lieutenants we have Plymouths, Fords, and Chevies; for majors and colonels, we have Dodges, Pontiacs, and Mercuries; for fat-ass generals we have Cadillacs and Lincolns."

The calling soldier demanded angrily, "Do you know who I am? I'm General George Patton."

"Oh," asked the soldier, "do you know who I am?"

"No, I don't," replied General Patton.

"Fine," said the soldier. "Goodbye, Fat-Ass."

262. FEAR OF AUTHORITY: A group of men arrived for Marine basic training at Parris Island, South Carolina. The drill instructor intimidated them thoroughly at the outset. "All right," he began. "Get this and get it straight. My name is Staff Sergeant Stone, and I'm even harder than my name."

He then strutted down the line of stiffened boys and asked the name of each in turn. Upon reaching the smallest one with his question, there was no answer. In a voice that would shake Gibraltar, he roared, "Are you just going to ignore me, Private? I said, 'What's your name?' "

The men could barely hear the almost tearful voice that answered: "Stonebreaker, sir."

263. UNCLEAR ORDERS: General Andrew Jackson (1767–1845), during the Battle of New Orleans, ordered: "Boys, elevate them guns a little lower."

264. UNCLEAR ORDERS: When some American airmen were training in the British Royal Air Force Parachute and Jungle Survival School at Changi, Singapore, they were advised: "Try to crash in June, July, or August, when there is more edible fruit about."

265. CLEAR ORDERS: Drill sergeant to recruits: "Wipe that opinion off your face."

266. LACK OF COMMUNICATION: All airmen going through basic training at the Lackland Air Force Base in California are urged to write frequent letters home. But they don't always do so. One such airman had to be called into the commander's office when this letter was received from his mother: "Dear Sir: I have not heard from my son for three weeks. If he is dead, please send his body to Route 1, Hugo, Oklahoma 74743."

267. And the last military story perhaps could be classified as USEFUL GENERAL RULES FOR ANY SITUATION: sergeant major's rule for men on duty in the officers' mess:

If it moves, salute it.

If it doesn't move, sweep it up.

If it's too big to sweep up, pick it up.

If it's too big to pick up, paint it.

Now let's get away from military "business" and into some more conventional aspects of commercial life. Maybe some people are glad they don't have to make money through free enterprise.

268. Two bums were lounging on a bench downtown when they saw a businessman walking by.

Bum 1: "What's he carrying in his briefcase?"

Bum 2: "Nothing but problems and troubles."

Speaking of problems and troubles, salespeople certainly have some.

269. A salesman, Mr. Gosner, was selling vacuum cleaners in a rural area. He was allowed to enter a farmhouse and show off his machine to Mrs. Fillmore. He was extolling its virtues and then reached into a bag and pulled out a handful of horse manure, which he scattered all over the carpet. Then he said to Mrs. Fillmore, "If this machine doesn't sweep up all this manure and have your carpet clean as a whistle, I'll eat it."

Mrs. Fillmore got up and headed for the kitchen.

"Where are you going?" asked Mr. Gosner.

"I'm going to get the salt and pepper. Our house isn't wired for electricity."

270. A businessman was having trouble with his sales. So he called in a consultant to give him an objective view and some good advice. After he had explained all of his plans and problems, he showed the consultant a map into which he had stuck brightly colored pins wherever he had a salesman. Then he said, "O.K., for a starter, what is the first thing we should do?"

"Well," said the consultant, "the first thing is to take those pins out of the map and stick them in the salesmen."

271. A real estate agent was showing a property to a prospective client, and he said, "There are advantages and disadvantages to the property."

"Please explain," said the client.

"Well, to the north is the gasworks, to the east a glue factory, to the south a fish and chips shop, and to the west a sewage farm. Those are the disadvantages."

"What are the advantages?" asked the client.

"You can always tell which way the wind is blowing," said the agent.

272. A couch salesman said to his hoped-for customer, "In case relatives should drop in unexpectedly, this couch absolutely cannot be turned into a bed."

273. An excellent salesman whose customers were fairly prosperous executives was asked how he managed to be so successful. "Well," he replied, "I always follow the cardinal rules: Know your product; make lots of calls; never take no for an answer."

"Yes," asked the questioner, "and what else?"

"Well," said the salesman, "I always miss a three-foot putt by two inches."

274. A life insurance agent made his spiel, and then he said, "But don't let me frighten you into a hasty decision. Sleep on it tonight. If you wake up tomorrow, let me know."

The telephone can have effects on selling.

275. The J. K. Kleinbard department store had an automatic answering machine. When you called it said, "Thank you for calling us at Kleinbard's. If you wish to order a product, press 1.

"If you need to ask about paying a bill, press 2.

"If you are calling to register a complaint, press 6769201478439.

"Thank you, and have a good day!"

276. Mabel Gilpin stopped by a local San Francisco bank and found the customer service clerk. She waited at the window for quite a while while the clerk chatted on the telephone with a friend.

Mrs. Gilpin, growing impatient and angry, pounded on the counter. Then the clerk said, "Hold on a minute—I'm being interrupted by a customer."

If we go a few thousand miles west from San Francisco, we may reach a remarkable nation called Japan. Here one of the main problems is not lack of motivation to work.

277. *Asahi Shinbun* is a Japanese newspaper with over eight million circulation. A couple of years ago (it may have changed slightly now) the paper had a "problem" quite different from that of the San Francisco bank.

All over the *Asahi* offices there were posters showing a fierce boss shouting, "If you come to work during vacation, you're fired!"

278. Mr. Jeffrey Mohler, head of a manufacturing company, told an eager but worried-looking employee, "I'm very sorry, Egbert, but if I let you take a two-hour lunch today, every worker whose wife gives birth to quadruplets will want one, too."

279. In a branch office of the J. G. Quadrant Company, one of the major problems was discipline. One of the employees of JGQ Co. violated a major company policy, so Stephen Brown, the manager, decided to make an example of the man. "Jones," he said, "I hereby tell you that you are suspended for three days without pay."

"Oh, Mr. Brown," responded Jones, "can you make it five days? I need a week off."

280. Of course, in business some people get a lot more than a week off—they're fired. The president of a small company said to a manager, "You're now manager emeritus."

"What does that mean?" asked the manager.

"It's Latin," explained the president. "*E* means 'exit' and *meritus* means 'You deserve it.' "

And what about nonhuman creatures and their influence in business?

281. On his desk, the president of a small company kept a bowl with several goldfish in it. People who came into his office noticed that he would pause during interviews and look fondly at the fish. One day an employee dared to ask him, "Mr. Nicholson, I'm amazed how fond you seem to be of those goldfish. Why?"

"Well," replied Nicholson, "it's refreshing to have something in the office that opens its mouth and doesn't ask for a raise."

282. The board of directors of a hard-pressed company appointed a stray dog as honorary vice president. When news of the appointment got out, the company spokesman explained: "Fido's ability to get along with anyone, his prompt response to a pat on the back, his interest in watching others work, his great knack for looking wise and saying nothing, make him a natural."

Two factors in business—even more important than dogs and goldfish—are the stock market and advertising. Here are two bits about Wall Street.

283. A wise, very experienced broker was asked by a friend, "What's the latest dope on Wall Street?"

The broker replied, "My son."

284. John Pierpont Morgan (1867–1943) was asked by a member of a Congressional committee before which he was appearing, "What's the market going to do? Can you answer that?"

"Yes," said Morgan.

All members of the committee leaned forward eagerly to hear the answer.

Morgan pronounced, "It's going to fluctuate."

And here are three advertising stories.

285. There is an English-language newspaper *China Daily*, published, mainly for tourists, in Beijing. Here is an ad that appeared in that paper:

These Chinese foods, especially offered by well-known Chinese cooks, will give you endless after-taste.

286. Two geese were flying south. A frog wanted to go along. So the two geese stretched a long blade of grass between them and said: "Grab ahold!"

The frog grabbed the grass with his mouth, and off flew the geese. Another bird came along and said, "Wow! That's a wonderful idea! Who thought of that?"

The proud and vainglorious frog said, "I did!"

When he opened his mouth, of course, he fell to his death.

Moral: When you have a good thing, keep your big fat mouth shut.

287. There were two store owners, Mr. Vanegal and Mr. Frimmee. They were at lunch, and Mr. Frimmee asked his colleague, "Is your advertising getting results?"

"It sure is," replied Mr. Vanegal. "Last week we advertised for a night watchperson. The next night we were robbed."

A part of business success is enterprise—probably free and private. Consider the following:

288. A 71-year-old woman, Mrs. Smallwood, had to call a furnace repairman. The man, after a quick inspection, put some oil into the motor and handed Mrs. Smallwood a bill for $70 for labor. "Labor!" exclaimed Mrs. Smallwood. "It took you only five minutes."

The repairman explained, "Our company has a minimum one-hour charge on every house call."

"Well," said Mrs. Smallwood, "I want my remaining fifty-five minutes of labor."

Then she handed the man a rake, and he spent the remaining fifty-five minutes in her yard bagging leaves.

289. Cyril Edwin Mitchinson (C.E.M.) Joad (1891–1953) was a prominent philosopher and radio personality in England. He had to spend a lot of time traveling from place to place on trains. Once he was at Reading, and an express train made an unscheduled stop there. Joad climbed aboard.

"Sir, you'll have to get off," a conductor told him. "This train does not stop here."

"In that case, don't worry," said Joad. "I'm not on it."

290. Speaking of enterprise, private/profit and maybe free, consider the triumphant words of the chairman of a wool manufacturing company: "Gentlemen, I have good news. Our research has developed a moth that will eat synthetics."

291. These days it's absolutely "in" to know how to use word processors and computers. But the manager of an aerospace company was a cyberphobic (one who is afraid of electronic devices). One day he entered his office and found a computer terminal set up next to his desk. "What's this?" asked the manager.

An engineer replied vigorously, "It's your new terminal, and it's just waiting for you to give it a command."

The manager glared at the computer and said, "Go away!"

And so we get ready to move to the next chapter: "Schools, Teachers—and Education?" Before we do, let's consider the effects on business of too much elegantist education.

292. Two business partners were quite successful, but had a hard time getting along together.

Partner 1: "I can't stand our partnership anymore."
Partner 2: "Why, what's the trouble?"
Partner 1: "The trouble is, you're too pretentious."
Partner 2: "Who, *moi?*"

Dear reader, are you *educated* enough to know that Partner 2 meant: "Who, me?" Whether you are or whether you aren't, you will enjoy the next chapter—*"oui, vous!"*

10.

Schools, Teachers— and Education?

Let's start with an example of an unexpected opportunity for education.

293. Julian Lowell Coolidge (1873–1954), professor of mathematics at Harvard, was lecturing one day. It was his habit to twirl his watch around on a chain as he spoke. Suddenly the chain broke and the watch sailed out over the students and landed, with a crash. Said Coolidge, with his strong Boston accent: "Gentlemen, that was an example of a puhfect puwabola."

Here's a perhaps less brilliant use of mathematical concepts.

294. There is an earth science class at Old Dominion University in Norfolk, Virginia. One topic was mapreading. The professor, according to the memory of Sandra Wadsworth, explained latitude, longitude, degrees, and minutes. Then he asked, trying to get practical, "Suppose I asked you to meet me for lunch at 23 degrees, 4 minutes north latitude and 45 degrees, 15 minutes east longitude . . . ?"

There was a confused silence, and then a voice said, "I guess you'd be eating alone."

295. But there was a twelfth grader in a school I know in Baltimore who, when she had learned about Albert Einstein's theory that space is curved, came to a remarkable conclusion. She said, "If it weren't for trees and mountains, I could see the back of my head."

Here's another somewhat latitudinal/longitudinal happening.

296. These days—thank God—more and more fathers are taking responsibility for baby care, but often it's hard for a dad unless his wife can help him draw from his own experience. When Mr. Nat Sample looked puzzled and frustrated by the task of putting on a diaper, his ingenious wife said, "O.K., Nat, it's pretty simple. The diaper is a baseball diamond. Bring second base to home plate and lay the baby between first and third. Now bring first, third, and home together and pin. And, by the way, be sure to dust home plate with a little talcum powder."

What a genius teacher Mrs. Sample was!

297. And speaking of cooperation and education, there is the story of a professor who had just completed a textbook on which he had been working for over two years. Also, his wife had just had a baby.

The professor went to see the baby, and he was delighted—but also very satisfied that his text was completed. As he came out of the hospital, one of his associates came up to him and said, "Congratulations, Professor!"

The professor replied, "Thank you very much. I never could have done it without the help of my wife and two graduate students."

But back to diapers and baseball. The position of things is important, as Mrs. Sample demonstrated in story 296. If things are out of position, there can be trouble—or comedy!

298. Five first graders marched out on the stage to welcome everyone at the PTA meeting. Each child carried a letter to make up the word "Hello." All took their correct positions except for one little boy who carried the letter *O*. He couldn't remember where to stand. He paused for a few minutes at the back of the stage, much to everyone's amusement. But he really brought down the house when he finally decided he belonged at the head of the group.

299. Benjamin Franklin (1706–1790) established an academy in 1751 that became the prestigious University of Pennsylvania, but he gets credit for the first joke at Harvard's expense. In 1722 he referred to the college as a place "where for want of suitable Genius, they learn little more than how to carry themselves handsomely and enter a Room genteelly (which might as well be acquired at a Dancing-school); and from whence they return after abundance of trouble and changes, as great Blockheads as ever, only more proud and self-conceited." Of course, Franklin's quip should be regarded with some suspicion, as it comes from a man who, despite lesser achievements, never made it to Harvard himself.

Ben Franklin never made it to Harvard, but there are worse things than that.

300. The following was written on the program of the New Mexico Arts and Crafts Fair: "Graduating with a B.F.A. from Northern Arizona University in 1976, Ernest Wilmeth turned to clay in 1982."

Here's hoping none of my readers turn to clay! However, here's a very unclaylike bit of education taken from *Learning to Bow* (Tickner and Fields, 1991), by Bruce S. Feiler, who spent a year in Japan as an American teacher.

301. The principal of the junior high school in Sano, Japan, believing that clothes helped form the character of students, hung an old student uniform outside his office with various warnings attached:

DON'T SHORTEN YOUR LEGS.

DON'T WEAR PLEATS.

DON'T PUT PURPLE LININGS IN YOUR POCKETS.

Above the limp clothing was written: A CLEAN UNIFORM MEANS A CLEAN HEART.

No doubt a clean heart is important for character and good education, but perhaps even more important is enthusiasm for learning—more and more.

302. Perhaps this story is about enthusiasm for *other* people's learning. Mrs. Ferraro was very proud of her sons and the colleges they attended, so she had decals displayed on the back window of her car: STANFORD: HARVARD: UNIVERSITY OF PENNSYLVANIA. But one day she got a flat tire and asked a passerby for help. The man replied, "Lady, you went to three colleges and you can't even change a tire?!"

303. Lack of enthusiasm for learning can get you into trouble. For example, Mrs. Selby confronted four of her students who didn't get to school till after lunch. "What happened?" she asked.

"Well, Mrs. Selby," replied one boy, "we had a flat tire."

"I'm sorry to hear that," said Mrs. Selby, "but you missed the test. Sit down right now at these desks well apart from each other."

The students did so.

"O.K.," said Mrs. Selby, "the first question is: Which tire was flat?"

304. On a college bird walk our instructor, Dr. Relman, identified the first birdcall. When the next call was heard, he asked, "What was that?"

"A chipmunk," one of the students volunteered.

"No," Dr. Relman said patiently. "That's a tufted titmouse."

"Well," said the student proudly, "at least I knew it wasn't a bird!"

305. Enthusiasm for learning can be important. A Harvard professor said, "If you have one dollar and I have one dollar and we exchange our dollars, we each still have one dollar. But if you have one idea and I have one idea and we exchange ideas, we each now have two ideas."

306. Requiring mere neatness in schoolwork can dampen enthusiasm. A second grader, Max, sometimes did his work sloppily. His teacher said, "Max, if you don't print neatly, you will not receive any credit for your work."

Max retorted, "Credit? I don't need credit. I've got VISA!"

307. The famous African-American singer Eartha Kitt, two of whose great songs were "I Want to Be Evil" and "C'est Si Bon," said, "I am learning all the time. The tombstone will be my diploma."

308. In the wilderness we need to keep learning. Boy Scout leader Bud Wilcox said to his troop as they took off on a long hike, "Remember, fellows, if you become lost in the woods at night, get your bearings from the sky."

"How do we do that, especially if it's cloudy?" asked one scout.

"Just look," said Wilcox. "A glow will indicate the nearest shopping center."

309. Some years ago, a dull student in London was taking a literacy test and not doing very well. The teacher looked at his paper and said, "The trouble with you is that you do not know the King's English."

The student glared at the teacher and retorted, "Of course he is!"

310. Miss Dewsnap, a rather proper teacher, took over a new fourth-grade class in the middle of the year. "Class," she said, "each of you will please tell me your name. We'll start at the left."

"Jule," replied the first boy.

"No, not Jule," said Miss Dewsnap. "It's Julius."

"O.K.," said Jule, "Julius."

Miss Dewsnap turned to the next boy. "And what's your name?"

"Billious," he replied.

311. Said an eager doctor to his patient, "You seem to be in fine health, but let's run a few tests. I'm sure we can find something wrong with you." (*Query*: bilious? Or maybe: "Bill you us.")

Here's a nobler view of learning and education.

312. Abraham Lincoln came from a very humble background (although it is *not* true, as a youngster wrote on a history test, "Abraham Lincoln was born in a log cabin which he built himself"). He was born in Kentucky and was entirely self-educated. Long before 1861, when he was elected President, a local person asked him, "Why do you read so much? An education won't help you to earn a living."

"I'm not educating myself to earn a living," Lincoln replied. "I'm trying to learn what to do with a living if ever I earn it."

We'll close the chapter on education with three stories about the "highest" areas of the subject: school principals, school boards, and money.

313. A very wise school principal said to some colleagues, "The only person who cannot refer to 'my school' is the head. It's a little like Jonah saying, 'My whale.'

"However," he continued, "Jonah came out all right."

314. Mark Twain said, "School boards are what the Lord made after He had practiced making idiots."

315. Vartan Gregorian was head of the New York Public Library from 1981 to 1988. He then left and in 1989 became president of Brown University in Providence, Rhode Island. After a very short time in office, he said to the board of the university: "Brown has been an institution that does more with less. Well, I'm here to tell you that we're out of less."

11.

History—Bunk, Perspective, or Truth?

316. Perhaps the most concise definition of history was spoken by the great American industrialist Henry Ford (1863–1947). His Model T sold over 15 million, and the Model A did even better. These are facts of history. But when Ford was on the witness stand in Mt. Clemens, Michigan, he stated during his libel suit against the *Chicago Tribune* (July 1919): "History is bunk."

317. Long before Henry Ford, the Anglo-Irish author Oliver Goldsmith (1730–1774) wrote in his famous *Citizen of the World*: "On whatever side we regard the history of Europe, we shall perceive it to be a tissue of crimes, follies, and misfortunes." Does *tissue* mean "a mesh of lies"? If so, Goldsmith would agree with Ford.

318. I suppose most of my readers would consider Western civilization to be a historical fact or set of facts and development. However, when a reporter asked the great Indian leader Mohandas Gandhi (1869–1948), known as Mahatma (great-souled), "What do you think of Western civilization?" he replied, "I think it would be a good idea."

319. Western civilization has produced a number of great celebrities. Many of them have large egos, and some of these write autobiographies. Sam Ewing wrote: "If you believe the past can't be changed, you haven't read a celebrity's autobiography."

Perhaps we've now dealt enough with the bunk part of this chapter. Let's consider perspective—a long, delightful subject.

320. The planet Earth, we human beings think, is a pretty large place—even heavy. Well, we should know that a neutron star is invisible but so dense that a teaspoon of it weighs about one billion tons.

321. Most people, when they think of dinosaurs, wonder what made them extinct. A much more amazing thing is that dinosaurs lived on Earth for 150 million years. What about *Homo sapiens*? According to archaeologists, we've been around about 300,000 years, and our predecessors, *Homo erectus*, about 1.5 million years. Given the things that we *sapienses* (is that a word?) are doing these days, would you be willing to bet that we'll last another 148 million years?

322. The Earth, this history-ridden planet, is about 4½ billion years old. That's hard for us earthlings to conceptualize. However, it is made easier by the Swiss-born naturalist, author, and teacher Louis Agassiz. At the start of each year, Agassiz would tell his students: "Gentlemen, the world is older than we have been taught to think. Its age is as if one were gently to rub a silk handkerchief across Plymouth Rock once a year until it were reduced to a pebble."

323. Galileo (1564–1642), the Italian astronomer, mathematician, and physicist who constructed the first astronomical telescope, wrote: "The sun, with all those planets revolving around it and dependent on it, can still ripen a bunch of grapes as if it had nothing else in the universe to do."

324. There are rocks and pebbles, and the sun and grapes—*and* civilization—but all of this was put in perspective by William James Durant (1885–1981), who wrote the 11-volume *The Story of Civilization.*

Will Durant said, "Civilization exists by geological consent: subject to change without notice."

325. We Earth people think that we and our history are pretty important. Consider this fact: If the world population of about 5.4 billion people were gathered together in one spot, with each person standing (not lying!) on a generous two-by-two patch of ground, we'd cover less than 800 square miles—about the size of Jacksonville, Florida.

We have to keep even very dramatic human events in perspective.

326. One of the most famous floods in American history was the Johnstown flood in Pennsylvania. It occurred in 1889, and about 2,200 people died.

Well, there was an old man who for much of his life bored people by relating in great detail how he had survived The Flood. Finally he died and went to Heaven. He met Saint Peter at the Pearly Gates:

Saint Peter: "Have you any request to make?"

Johnstown man: "I would like to tell how I survived the Johnstown Flood."

Saint Peter: "That can be arranged."

So the great day came and there was an audience of more than 10,000 there. Just before the Johnstown man was to start, Saint Peter leaned over and said, "There's just one thing I think I should tell you. Noah is in the audience."

327. The Welsh are a splendid people with magnificent voices. They also are proud of their past. One Welsh family in Llandavery has a pedigree that covers five large skins of parchment. In the middle of the third page is a note in the margin: "About this time the world was created."

Sometimes even the wisest of us can go far wrong as we consider history and then look forward to the future.

328. Lord Ernest Rutherford (1871–1937) was a great physicist and chemist and became a Nobel laureate in 1908. He was the first person to split atomic nuclei, in 1933. He wrote then: "The energy produced by the breaking down of the atom is a very poor kind of thing. Anyone who expects a source of power from the transformation of the atom is talking moonshine."

329. In his *Day of Infamy* Walter Lord reports that in the program for the Army–Navy game, November 29, 1941, this caption appeared under a photograph of the USS *Arizona*: "It is significant that despite the claims of air enthusiasts, no battleship has yet been sunk by bombs."

Eight days later, the *Arizona* sank at Pearl Harbor.

330. In the 18th century the French philosopher and

author François Voltaire (1694–1778) said that the church was a dying institution. He predicted it would not last over 50 years.

At the end of that time, the house in Paris where he had made the prediction was being used as a center for the distribution of the Bible.

331. A hot trend these days is computers, word processors, and all sorts of cybernetic devices. Perhaps we should have a sense of perspective about this. Consider a rod of graphite encased in wood, first used in the 16th century. It's called a pencil. Here are some of the marvels about it:

It can write underwater.

It can write in outer space.

A standard 7¼-inch pencil can draw a line
  35 miles long.

It can write 45,000 words.

It can scratch your back.

It can prop open a window.

It can lubricate a stuck zipper.

It can pin up long hair.

Pencils can be bought for 49 cents a dozen.

SO: Pencil all that in!

332. Mark Twain (1835–1910), who knew a good deal about money, life, and people, wrote: "All you need in this life is ignorance and confidence, and then success is sure."

333. Adela Rogers St. Johns was one of America's great writers, and she lived to be 94 years old. She made the most of each day and laughed at "the ravages of time," as she called them. She was a Mark Twain admirer and quoted him thus: "Wrinkles should merely indicate where the smiles have been."

Perhaps a good way to deal with life and with history is to remember our relationship with things of the past. It may help to make us more respectful, more humorous, and more enjoyable.

334. Jonas Edward Salk, who developed the vaccine against polio, said, "The work I have been able to do depended on the research of men and women whose names remain unknown but whose labors make possible my work." And Sir Isaac Newton (1642–1727), who discovered the universal law of gravitation and began the development of calculus, among other great accomplishments, said, "If I have been able to see farther than others, it was because I stood on the shoulders of giants."

And speaking of relationships with great people—

335. Senator Daniel Inouye of Hawaii gave a talk on "Our Kinship with the British People." During the question period that followed, someone asked, "Senator, how could you possibly be a kin of Britons?"

Inouye replied, "My great-great-great-great-grandfather ate Captain Cook."

336. The Fourth of July is one of our most important national holidays. A few years ago, a group of Friends (Quakers) was holding an international seminar on Orcas Island, one of the San Juan Islands off northwest Washington. One British Friend said, "You Americans call it Independence Day. We British prefer the term Good Riddance Day." And this reminds me that when my wife and I spent a year in England, we were asked where we came from. I usually said, "Philadelphia—that's where we declared our independence from the British."

More than once the reply was, "Oh, yes, and I understand you've been going downhill ever since."

337. Another way to relate to countries is through their antiques and relics. In Greece, a tourist group had been out shopping. One woman came running back to her group shouting, "Look what I got!"

"What is it?" they asked.

The woman replied, "The very cup from which Socrates drank the hemlock!"

"Well, that's wonderful!" exclaimed another member. "But are you sure it's authentic?"

"Of course," said the woman. "When they dug it up it was marked 399 B.C."

338. But touring ancient countries can be wearisome, as demonstrated by a traveler in Greece. He said to his group after a long day, "One more ruin and I'll be one, too."

339. One of the most famous ruins in the world is the Great Sphinx. During a class at a well-known university, the professor was challenging his students.

Professor: "All right, Larry, can you tell us who built the Great Sphinx?"

Larry: "I did know, Professor, but I've forgotten."

Professor: "Great guns, what a calamity! The only man living who knows—and he has forgotten!"

The U.S.A. is not—for us European- or African- or Asian-based people, at least—an "ancient country," and the *real* history of our area did not begin with the "discoveries" of Columbus. Here's a bit of evidence.

340. Many of our present states got their names from Native Americans and their languages. Here are some. Can you figure them out? Alibamu, Arizonac, Quonoktacuk, Edahoe, Illini, Kanza, Massawaschuasch, Missisipi, Missiuri, Tanasee, Texia, Arkansea, and Ute.

The Europeans who immigrated here met (and, over

the years, greatly damaged) many civilizations already established. Consider the following:

341. *Young boy*: "My mom said that her family came over on the *Mayflower*. And my dad told her that he already knew that."

Listening neighbor: "How did he know that?"

Young boy: "Because Dad said her family always arrives uninvited and stays forever."

342. In New Mexico, there is a paper called the *Tuidoso News*. In 1991 it published a photo with this caption: "Ellen Hightower's first grade class at Nob Hill performed a short recital called 'America.' The program honored early American settlers and the Indians that beheaded them."

Here's another "Indian" story. It may not be "humorous," but it is certainly wise.

343. In 1855 Chief Sealth (from whom Seattle got its name) wrote this letter to President Franklin Pierce (1804–1869).

"There is no quiet place in the white man's cities. No place to hear the unfurling of leaves in spring or the rustle of insects' wings. But perhaps it is because I am a savage and do not understand. The clatter only seems to insult the ears. And what is there to life if a man cannot hear the lonely cry of the whippoorwill or the arguments of the frogs around a pond at night? I am a red man and I do not understand.

The Indian prefers the soft sound of the wind darting over the face of a pond, and the smell of the wind itself, cleansed by a midday rain, or scented with the pinyon pine.

Even the white man, whose God walks and talks with him as a friend, cannot be exempt from the common destiny. We may be brothers after all, we shall see. One thing we know, which the white man may one day discover—Our God is the same God. You may think now that you own Him as you wish to own our land; but you cannot. He is the God of man and His compassion is equal for the red man and the white.

The Earth is precious to Him, and to harm the Earth is to heap contempt on its creator: The whites, too, shall pass, perhaps sooner than all the other tribes. Continue to contaminate your bed and you will one night suffocate in your own waste. This we know. The Earth does not belong to man: man belongs to the Earth. This we know. All things are connected like the blood which unites one family. All things are connected. Whatever befalls the Earth befalls the sons of the earth. Man did not weave the web of life; he is merely a strand in it. Whatever he does to the web he does to himself."

Who runs "the Earth"? Another way of putting it is: What does history have to work with? Here are three answers—sort of—to those profound questions:

344. E. M. Forster (1879–1970), the great English novelist and author of *A Passage to India*, wrote: "I believe in aristocracy—if that is the right word, and if a democrat may use it. Not an aristocracy of power, based on rank and influence, but an aristocracy of the sensitive, the considerate, and the plucky. Its members are to be found in all nations and classes, and all through the ages, and there is an understanding between them when they meet. They represent the true human tradition, the one permanent victory of our queer race over cruelty and chaos. Thousands of them perish in obscurity, a few are great names. They are sensitive for others as well as for themselves, they are considerate without being fussy, their pluck is not swankiness but the power to endure, and they can take a joke."

345. John Dewey (1859–1952), one of America's greatest educators and philosophers, rejected authoritarian teaching and was a major influence in "progressive education." He didn't have a very high opinion of conventional religion and wrote: "While saints are engaged in introspection, burly sinners run the world."

346. George Santayana (1863–1952), a great American philosopher, taught at Harvard (1890–1912) and then moved to Europe. He considered religion an imaginative creation of real value but without absolute significance. He wrote thus about what history has to work with: "In human nature, generous impulses are occasional or reversible. They are spent in childhood, in dreams, in extremities, and they are often weak or soured in old age. They form amiable interludes like tearful sentiments in a ruffian, or they are pleasant self-deceptive hypocrisies acted out, like civility to strangers, because such is in society the path of least resistance. Strain the situation, however, dig a little beneath the surface, and you will find a ferocious, persistent, profoundly selfish man."

347. "Profoundly selfish," are we? Well, at least profoundly self-centered as evidenced by a juror at a recent trial who said to a fellow juror: "I don't listen to the evidence. I like to make up my own mind."

But there is an element of unselfishness in human beings.

348. A married couple, both in their late eighties, went to an attorney and said, "We want a divorce."

"A divorce—at your age?!" exclaimed the attorney. "Why did you wait so long?"

The about-to-be ex-wife replied, "We wanted to wait until our children were dead."

A sense of direction and upward looking are necessary for us to deal with the major problems that have troubled our human societies throughout history.

349. Harry Emerson Fosdick (1878–1969), the famous Modernist clergyman leader of the Riverside Church in New York City, said that "when we were children and had to cross a creek on a single log, we learned a procedure which helped. If we looked down at the swirling water below, the chances were more than even that we would fall in. But if we picked a tree on the opposite bank which was in line with the log, and held our heads up to look at it, we could walk across without mishap."

The importance of keeping a sense of direction while threatened by swirling waters is perhaps a good way to end this chapter on history—and a good one to lead to the next chapter on government and politics.

12.

Government and Politics

Brown University may have been "out of less" in 1989, but there's one thing that the governments are never out of, and that is regulations.

350. James Anthony Froude (1818–1894), the English historian, said, "If medicine had been regulated three hundred years ago by Act of Parliament; if there had been Thirty-nine Articles of Physic, and every licensed practitioner had been compelled, under pains and penalties, to compound his drugs by the prescriptions of Henry the Eighth's physician, Dr. Butts, it is easy to conjecture in what state of health the people of this country would at present be found."

351. According to the *Harvard Magazine*, "Some experts view the Harvard Charter of 1650 (responsible for the structure of governance by a Corporation and

Board of Overseers) as a work of considerable comic achievement. They argue that the charter—which stipulates that 'the President, Fellowes, & Schollers ... shall be exempted from all civil offices, militarie exercises, or services ... and shall be free from all Country taxes or rates whatsoever'—is without exception the most glorified tax shelter of the early modern era. Never, they claim, has there been such an efficient attempt to dodge taxes, civil service, and the draft all in one document."

352. Someone at the Food and Drug Administration was heard to say, "If laughter is the best medicine, shouldn't we be regulating it?"

353. There was a man who didn't have a first name or a middle name. He was always known as R. B. Jones. He got along fine until he went to work for a government agency. The government's regulations insist on full names on all official forms, like payroll and personnel listings. Someone, however, recognized R.B.J.'s right to his name and so indicated on basic forms: "R(only) B(only) Jones."

But it didn't work. When R.B.J. got his paycheck it was made out to "Ronly Bonly Jones."

354. Probably all of us have great difficulty with the language in the regulations of the Internal Revenue Code. Here's an example: "For purposes of paragraph (3), an organization described in paragraph (2) shall be deemed to include an organization described in section 501(c)(4), (5) or (6) which would be described in paragraph (2) if it were an organization described in section 501(c)(3)."

355. A couple of years ago, I received a copy of an official government document from someone who liked collecting examples of humorous—and maybe tragic—human behavior. It refers to the now famous and practically ignored Gramm-Rudman Act to balance the U.S. budget. This act was named for its sponsors, Phil Gramm of Texas and Warren B. Rudman of New Hampshire.

Here is the document (slightly shortened):

Reference or Official Symbol	Subject		
MEPCE-STP	Implementation of The Gramm-Rudman Budget Reduction Act		

TO	FROM	DATE	CMT 1
All Federal Employees	MEPCE-STP	19 Sept. 1988	

1.   As a result of the reduction in money budgeted for government purposes, we must cut down on our number of personnel. Under this plan, older employees will go on early retirement, thus permitting the retention of younger people. . . .

2.   Therefore, a program . . . will be placed into effect immediately. The program will be known as RAPE (Retire Aged Persons Early). Employees who are RAPED will be given the opportunity to work other jobs within the system. Provided they are being RAPED, they can request a review of their employment records. . . . This phase of the reduction program is called SCREW (Survey of Capabilities of Retired Early Workers).

3.   All employees who have been RAPED or SCREWED may apply for a new reemployment eligibility service. This service will be called SHAFT (Study by Higher Authority Following Termination). Current regulations state that employees may only be RAPED once and SCREWED twice, but they may get the SHAFT as many times as Congress may deem appropriate.

4.   If an employee meets all of the above requirements, he/she will be entitled to get HERPES (Half Earnings of Retired Persons Entitlement Stipend). HERPES is considered a bonus plan, as those employees with HERPES can no longer be RAPED or SCREWED by the government. RAPED personnel may also get AIDS (Assistance for Immediate Displaced Services). Since AIDS has serious implications, one should request this service only once.

5.   Employees can enhance their retention prospects by signing up for additional training. It is

now, and always has been, the policy of the federal government to ensure all employees are well trained through our Special High Intensity Training (SHIT). We have given our employees more SHIT than any other organization in the country. . . .

5.   To ensure equal treatment of all federal employees, only Congress will be exempt from the above program.

[signature]

356. The widow of a dead man filed a tax return for him in 1991. The Internal Revenue Service sent a letter addressed to the dead man. It said: "Please provide your date of death."

357. Speaking of (and maybe *to*) dead people, consider the following, published by that superexcellent paper *The Philadelphia Inquirer* on March 8, 1992:

"Nothing can screw up your life-style like dying.

Just ask a guy who died last month in Greenville, S.C.

Some of you might be asking how you can ask a dead guy anything.

Well, his being dead didn't stop the Greenville County Department of Social Services from sending him a letter.

'Your food stamps will be stopped effective March 1992 because we received notice that you passed

away,' the letter to the dead guy said. 'May God
bless you.'

Despite the nice touch at the end, the letter made it
sound as if the decision to stop food stamps was final.

But not all public agencies are cold. The department offered the dead guy hope for the future.

'You may reapply if there is a change in your cir-
cumstances,' the letter said.

At first, Al Palanza Jr., brother of the dead guy,
read the letter and said he was disgusted. Later, he
found it funny. He called it 'living proof of how
screwed up the system is.'

Robin Kubler, the county's social services director,
said it's not her system that's screwed up. She said
the form letter was generated by a computer system.

And the 'May God Bless you'? That was added by
a caseworker, she said, to soften the statement."

Government regulations exist all over the world. Who
says God's in charge?!—despite the Ten Commandments. (Actually there were over 500 Commandments
set forth as the Laws of Moses.)

358. A popular Chinese saying is: *Lu fen dn,
biaomiam guang*, which means: "Shiny on the
outside—just like donkey droppings." In more practical words, this means: "The government has patched
over problems by constructing a few nice buildings."

Now let's go to Los Angeles, Moscow, and Germantown (Philadelphia), Pennsylvania. Who says we're not world-minded?!

359. The *Los Angeles Times* reported the following: "CHEATING POLICE: Eleven National City police officers were caught cheating on a promotion exam. However, no disciplinary action was taken against them because they had not been specifically instructed not to cheat."

360. In 1957 a reporter drove the 600 miles from Brest, France, to Moscow, then-USSR. He was given a copy of the official Rules of the Road by a Russian, which were: 1. While being at the wheel, you should always be capable of driving the car. 2. When necessary, the car should be stopped to avoid an accident. 3. Blowing horn in the city of Moscow is prohibited.

361. In 1988 a friend of mine reported on some problems he was having discovering what purchases for Germantown Friends Meeting were tax-exempt. He asked about the Pennsylvania taxability of various items. Materials for the roof?—no, not taxable; hymnals?—no, not taxable; toilets?—yes, taxable because "toilets are not a church function."

Regulations are certainly a part of government, and they lead to procedures.

362. P. J. O'Rourke wrote a delightful, if a bit sarcastic, book about government titled *A Parliament of Whores* (1991). In it he says that "government is so tedious that sometimes you wonder if it isn't being boring on purpose. Maybe they're *trying* to put us to sleep so we won't notice what they're doing."

363. In a rural area, a highway department truck stopped on the road. A worker got out and dug a large hole in the ditch. Next, after a few minutes, a second worker got out, filled in the hole, and tamped down the dirt. Then they drove on for about fifty yards and repeated the procedure. They did this exact same thing about six times.

A farmer who had been watching walked over and asked, "What are you doing?"

"Oh, sir," one of the workers said, "we're on a highway beautification project."

"Beautification!?" exclaimed the farmer. "What's so beautiful about all those filled-in holes?"

"Well, you see," said the worker, "the man who plants the trees is out sick today."

Is it any wonder that people get disillusioned or even disgusted with government? For example:

364. A few years ago, the Washington headquarters of the Democratic National Committee had a big problem: They had a flood of calls on one of a block of twenty telephone lines. Why? Their number was

202-333-8768, but word got out that if you dialed 202-FED UP68, you reach the headquarters.

365. *Teacher:* "Albert, what is the size of the Democratic Party?"

Albert: "About five feet two inches."

Teacher: "Idiot! I mean how many members does it have? How do you get five feet two inches?"

Albert: "Well, my father is six feet tall, and every night he puts his hand to his chin and says, 'I've had the Democratic Party up to here!' "

366. While we're on the subject of youngsters and political figures, you should know that the former Secretary of Housing and Urban Development, Jack Kemp, was giving a speech to a group of U.S. Catholic leaders. He said that his four-year-old grandson had introduced him as "a very important public serpent."

Before we go on to other stories about people in government and politics, I should emphasize that just because many of the items in this chapter play upon the nutty, foolish, and even corrupt behavior of politicians, almost all people in government whom I know or have known personally are hardworking, honest, very intelligent people. And I wouldn't want their jobs!

Here are some serious opinions about politics and

politicians. And, don't forget, all nations do need policies.

367. There is no more perfect endowment in man than political virtue.

PLUTARCH (46–120)

368. The conduct of a wise politician is ever suited to the present posture of affairs. Often by forgoing a part, he saves the whole, and by yielding in a small matter secures a greater.

PLUTARCH

369. He serves his party best who serves his country best.

RUTHERFORD B. HAYES (1822–1893)

370. Public officers are servants and agents of the people to execute laws which the people have made.

GROVER CLEVELAND (1837–1908)

371. Politics I conceive to be nothing more than the science of the ordered progress of society along the line of greatest usefulness and convenience to itself.

WOODROW WILSON (1856–1924)

372. One of the great things about the United States is that we can distinguish rhetoric from reality.

JOHN KENNETH GALBRAITH (1908–)

373. A friend of mine sent me the following: "When government officials decide to talk turkey, it usually ends up as gobbledegook."

374. During a California senatorial contest many years ago, one of the candidates was being badly maligned. A voter wired him thus: "A report receiving wide circulation here that your children have not been baptized. Telegraph denial immediately."

The reply came back: "Sorry to say, report is correct. I have no children."

375. You have doubtless heard of former Vice President J. Danforth Quayle and former President George Herbert Walker Bush. During their term of office, someone asked, "Why won't they allow dogs on the White House grounds?" The answer was, "Because they pee on the bushes and chase the quails."

376. Another not very pro-Bush statement was that "he was born on third base and thought he'd hit a triple." So it pays to be a Yale graduate and head a Texas oil-drilling company?

377. *Important businessman:* "I'd like to give you a new car."

Politician: "Oh, I can't accept that; it would be bribery."

Businessman: "O.K., I'll *sell* you a car for $50."

Politician: "Fine! In that case, I'll take two."

Now let's look at two examples of politics and government: England and France.

378. Queen Victoria (1819–1901), who reigned over England longer than any other monarch, said of four-times Prime Minister William Gladstone, "He speaks to me as if I were a public meeting."

379. In his younger days, French statesman Georges Clemenceau (1841–1929), popularly known as "the Tiger," fought a number of duels. Once he was to duel in a Parisian suburb. He bought a one-way ticket.

"A one-way ticket?" said his second. "Are you pessimistic?"

"Not at all," replied Clemenceau. "I always use my opponent's return ticket."

And he lived over 88 years!

380. Let's turn to the most important—well, *nearly* most important—factor for politicians to get elected. To be elected, you have to be alive!

381. Former President George Bush (1924–) was once asked which presidential speech he most admired. He replied, "It was the one Teddy Roosevelt had in his pocket that helped cushion the blow of a would-be assassin's bullet."

(Actually, Theodore Roosevelt [1858–1919] had a good reason to fear assassination. His predecessor, William McKinley [1843–1901], was assassinated by anarchist Leon Czolgosz, and Roosevelt himself, on October 14, 1912, was the target of an assassination attempt by schoolkeeper John N. Schrank. Roosevelt was running for another term as President [the third party: "Bull Moose"]. The would-be assassin's bullet was deflected by a glasses case in Teddy's pocket, not a speech document.)

382. Speaking of Presidents, there was a movie released in 1964: *The Best Man*. In it, two major actors, Henry Fonda and Cliff Robertson, acted as two candidates for President of the United States. A United Artists executive replied to the suggestion that Ronald Reagan be considered for one of the roles: "Reagan doesn't have the presidential look," he said.

383. John F. Kennedy was helped in his political career by his father, Joseph Patrick Kennedy, who was a man of considerable wealth and influence. One day during the time JFK was running for President, he received this telegram from his father:

DON'T BUY A SINGLE VOTE MORE THAN NECESSARY. I'LL BE DAMNED IF I'M GOING TO PAY FOR A LANDSLIDE.

384. On the campaign trail, an Illinois State Representative mailed a letter to hoped-for contributors. It stated that he had won "special recognition" by *Chicago Magazine*. Actually, the magazine called him one of Illinois's ten worst legislators.

Oh, to be elected!

385. In the *Oakland and Piedmont* the following was published: "In 1984 incumbent Don Excell died a month before the election, and in 1988 he did not have any opposition."

386. James Otis wrote in 1763: "Taxation without representation is tyranny." He was referring to the acts of the English Parliament to place duties on imports like tea.

Recently a politician seeking election stated in his platform for reelection: "I favor representation without taxation."

Sometimes a person's religious affiliation will affect people's voting, as also will the emphasis that person puts on certain words.

387. Thomas D. McBride, who died in 1965, was Attorney General of Pennsylvania in 1956. Also, he was an eminent Philadelphia lawyer; chancellor of the Philadelphia Bar Association; member of the board of the American Civil Liberties Union; on the Pennsylvania Supreme Court; and a member of the Roman Catholic Church.

When he was running for election to the Supreme Court, he told a group of friends that he was feeling a bit discouraged.

"Why?" they asked.

"Because," said McBride, "the Protestants won't vote for me because I'm a lousy *Catholic*, and the Catholics won't vote for me because I'm a *lousy* Catholic."

Note: Despite—or perhaps because of—all this, he won the election.

13.

Speakers and Writers— to Say or Not to Say

In *Hamlet*, Shakespeare wrote, "Brevity is the soul of wit." Perhaps this is a good way to begin a chapter on speaking and writing.

388. Back in 1975, a sales representative whose name I don't know made the following speech to a large conference. "I dictated my talk to my secretary and told her to cross out anything she thought was dull and uninteresting.

"And so, in conclusion—"

389. A retired insurance friend of mine told me of the first sentence in a speech he heard at a convention breakfast: "Before I start talking, I want to say something."

As he remembers it, both the saying and the talking were delightfully brief.

390. Yet another brief speech was given by Secretary of State William Maxwell Evarts (1818–1901) to the guests at a Thanksgiving dinner. He began: "You have been giving your attention to a turkey stuffed with sage; you are now about to consider a sage stuffed with turkey." He got a good laugh and stopped speaking shortly thereafter.

391. George Bernard Shaw was at a dinner party, and his host asked if he would make some remarks on the sexual relations of men and women. Shaw agreed, and at the appropriate time, rose and said, "Ladies and gentlemen, it gives me great pleasure," and then sat down.

392. A young girl whom I taught years ago wrote the following review: "This book tells more about penguins than I am interested in knowing."

393. Novelist Sinclair Lewis (1885–1951) was lecturing to a group of college students who were planning literary careers. He started by asking, "How many of you really intend to be writers?"

Every hand went up.

"In that case," said Lewis, folding up his notes, "my advice to you is: Go home and write."

With that, he left the room.

394. Mark Twain (1835–1910): "I was gratified to be able to answer promptly. I said, 'I don't know.' "

Here are four thoughts about brevity, or lack of it:

395. If a thing goes without saying, let it.

396. The speaker who rises to the occasion should know when to sit down.

397. The reason we make a long story short is so that we can tell another.

398. What many orators lack in depth, they give you in length.

399. As a speaker, I know how dull it is to hear a long introduction. Nobody ever expressed that feeling better than Alabama Senator Howel Heflin. He started a speech to the American Institute of Bankruptcy by saying: "I believe that was the most comprehensive introduction I have ever received. You omitted perhaps one thing—that in 1974 I had a hemorrhoidectomy."

400. In March 1992, at Harvard, Professor of Government Harvey Mansfield, Jr., brilliantly and briefly introduced speaker Camille Paglia, author of *Sexual Personae*, whose subject was "What's Wrong with Harvard?" Mansfield said: "Professor Paglia is an enemy of the namby-pamby, the hoity-toity, and the artsy-fartsy. She fires back when fired upon—or sometimes even sooner. She restores the art of invective to the academy. There are places where angels fear to tread, but there is nowhere that Professor Paglia fears to tread."

Back to brevity.

401. Someone asked what he thinks is a very cogent question. "Why is it that a lawyer writes a five-thousand-word document and then calls it a 'brief'?"

402. Rudyard Kipling (1865–1936) could be brief.

An American wrote Kipling, "I hear that you are selling your work at one dollar a word. Enclosed is one dollar. Please send me a sample."

Kipling kept the dollar and replied, "Thanks."

403. Quaker (Friends) Meetings for Worship are based on silence, and anyone may speak as he or she feels "moved" to. This sometimes leads to a person speaking at great length. (See my book *Quaker Meeting: a Risky Business*, Dorrance Publishing Co., 1991. To order call 1-800-788-7654.) After one such utterance, a witty Friend rose and said, "If some Friends would use temperance in their speaking, others would not have to practice total abstinence."

404. Speaking too long is a problem in Quaker Meetings, but another one is speaking inaudibly. In a 1992 *Bulletin* from Charlbury Meeting, near Oxford, this item appears.

"*Mumbled Ministry*. The new bare floor of the Meeting House has added an echo to the list of difficulties of those who are hard of hearing. So can we all make an effort in future to swallow our diffidence and not our words?"

405. In a Meeting for Worship at a Friends School, a teacher recited this message:
   "A wise old owl sat in our oak,
   The more he heard, the less he spoke;
   The less he spoke, the more he heard.
   Why aren't we all like this wise old bird?"

The next story takes us nicely from the subject of brevity or silence to that of opinions about people's writing.

406. Victor Hugo (1802–1885), the French poet, dramatist, and novelist, had submitted the manuscript of *Les Misérables* to his publisher and wanted to know how he liked it. He wrote: "?" The publisher replied: "!"

Now, that's brevity! And also an opinion.

Moving on into opinions about various writings, I should first say (as the author of 54 published books that have sold over 22 million copies) that I've had my share of rejection letters.

407. Many, many writers submit manuscripts to publishers. Here's a typical response.

REEJECKSHUN UNPUBLISHERS, INC.
000 Getoutta Heer Avenue
Grouchmouth, Pennsylvarkasass 00000-0000

Eric W. Jokesperson
99999 Stupidity Alley
Bumblebum, New Nevada 11111-1111

Dear Mr. Jokesperson:

Thank you for allowing us to see your work *How to Fail on All Occasions: a Handbook for Chronic Dopes.* Much as we admire your work, we regret to say that it does not meet our present publishing needs.

We wish you well as you seek a more appropriate publisher.

Sincerely yours,

I.Q. Minus
Ass. Ass. Deacquisitions Editor

408. An author received the following glorious rejection slip from a Chinese publishing firm: "We read your manuscript with boundless delight. By the sacred ashes of our ancestors we swear that we have never dipped into a book of such overwhelming mastery. If we were to publish this book, it would be impossible in the future to issue any book of a lower standard. As it is unthinkable that within the next 10,000 years we shall find its equal, we are, to our great regret, compelled to return this too divine work and beg you a thousand times to forgive our action."

409. Oscar Wilde (1854–1900) said about the novelist Henry James, "He writes fiction as if it were a painful duty."

410. Groucho Marx (1895–1977) received a copy of S. J. Perelman's first book, *Strictly from Hunger*. (Perelman later wrote the scripts for several Marx Brothers films.) Wrote Groucho to Perelman: "From the moment I picked your book up until I laid it down, I was convulsed with laughter. Someday I intend reading it."

411. Rudyard Kipling (1865–1936) was an extraordinarily successful writer. However, early in his career he was fired from his job as a reporter for the *San Francisco Examiner*. The editor who dismissed him said, "This isn't a kindergarten for amateur writers. I'm sorry, Mr. Kipling, but you just don't know how to use the English language."

412. The American writer Wilson Mizner (1876–1933) knew a good deal about Hollywood and its professional inhabitants—and also the romances that flourished (or floundered) there. He said: "Some of the greatest love affairs I've known have involved one actor—unassisted."

413. Charles Lamb (1775–1834) was an outstanding English essayist and poet. Once, while he was giving a lecture on his work, a loud hiss came forth from somewhere in the audience. There was a brief silence. Then Lamb said simply, "There are only three things that hiss—a goose, a snake, and a fool. Come forth and be identified."

414. Besides hissing, there are other ways of registering lack of enthusiasm for speeches. At a large sales conference meeting, at the end of the first speech, about half the audience walked out. At the end of the second speech, everybody else walked out, except for the third speaker and one other person. The third speaker went to the podium and said, "Are you sure you want to stay? If you leave, I won't have to make this speech."

The person replied, "I'm the last speaker."

415. Joseph Addison (1672–1719) was an extraordinarily able English essayist, poet, and statesman. However, he was a failure as a public speaker. From 1708 to 1719, he served in the House of Commons. At one session he tried to address the House: "Mr. Speaker, I conceive—I conceive, Sire—Sire, I conceive . . ." He was at this point interrupted by a member who quipped: "The right honorable Secretary of State has conceived thrice, and brought forth nothing."

416. Speaking of bringing forth nothing, Mark Twain (1835–1910) gave us these words of wisdom: "The right word may be effective, but no word was ever as effective as a rightly timed pause."

417. An almost universal subject of literary comment and criticism is William Shakespeare (1564–1616). At one time, Charles Lamb was talking with William

Wordsworth about Shakespeare and said, "I could write like Shakespeare if I had a mind to."

Wordsworth replied, "So, you see, it's the mind that's wanting."

418. One of the classic disputes about English literature is whether or not Shakespeare, considered the greatest of all playwrights, actually wrote all of the now classic poems and plays ascribed to him. Mark Twain had the last word on this. He butted into the discussion of a group of scholars to say, "It wasn't William Shakespeare who really wrote these plays, but another Englishman who was born on the same day at the same hour as he, and who died on the same day, and, to carry the coincidences still further, was also named William Shakespeare."

An interesting question—and a complex, unanswerable one—is, what makes, or how do you become, a good writer?

419. Aggressive self-promotion may be one of the ways. Recently at a convention of the Romance Writers of America, where most of the attendees were women, a man was seen walking about the large hotel lobby wearing a T-shirt with two messages on it. On the front it said: "My wife writes romance novels." On the back: "And I do the research."

420. Possibly another way is to make sure that you don't misspell words (although copy editors are excellent correctors, *and* there is no correlation between the ability to spell and a person's I.Q.). Many modern writers use a personal computer or word processor including a "spell check." The trouble is that spell checks can't deal with homonyms—words that sound alike but have different meanings.

A friend of mine sent me this verse on the subject:

I have a spelling checker,
It came with my PC;
It plainly marks four my revue
Mistakes I cannot sea.
I've run this poem threw it,
I'm sure your please too no,
Its letter perfect in it's weigh,
My checker tolled me sew.

421. Dorothy Parker (1893–1967) and Robert Benchley (1889–1945), both famous, witty writers, used to work for *Vanity Fair*. When they left the magazine, they went into the free-lance writing business together. On the door of their small office was written:

THE UTICA FORGE & TOOL COMPANY

BENCHLEY AND PARKER, PRESIDENTS

Their cable address was "Parkbench."

Later, in telling a friend about the tiny office, Parker said, "One cubic foot less of space and it would have constituted adultery."

422. There are other kinds of offices in which writers succeed. One of those belonged to the six-foot-one American novelist Theodore Dreiser (1871–1945), an immense, grandiose space furnished with oversize chairs. They were intended to diminish the person sitting in them. However, when the five-foot-one journalist, essayist, and linguist H. L. Mencken (1880–1956) visited Dreiser in 1908, he was not at all intimidated. Dreiser later wrote about Mencken's visit: "With the sangfroid of a Caesar or a Napoleon he made himself comfortable . . . and beamed on me with the confidence of a smirking fox about to devour a chicken."

423. Another way to succeed—or maybe fail—as a writer, and probably a speaker, too, is to get a book described thus in *Writer's Digest, List of Writing Guides: How to Write Fast (While Writing Well)*, by David Fryxell—"A practical, hands-on guide to organization, speed, concentration, problem solving, and creativity—for all type of writers."

424. There was a time when authors wrote their scripts by hand. Such was the situation of the British clergyman and writer Sydney Smith (1771–1845). He was successful and wrote many books. But he admitted that his handwriting was "lousy"—to use a modern meaning of an old word. Here's how he described it: "My writing is as if a swarm of ants, escaping from an ink bottle, had walked over a sheet of paper without wiping their legs." (Smith could insult other people's work as well as his own. He said of Sir Thomas B. Macaulay [1800–1859], the author of *History of England*: "He not only overflowed with learning, but stood in the slop.")

Another way to succeed as a writer is to have a fine ability to use metaphors.

425. Edward Lawrie Tatum (1909–1975), the famous American geneticist, said of a colleague: "His ear was so sensitive he could hear a mosquito pee on a bale of cotton." And of another person, he said, "He didn't spend *any* money. He was as tight as the instep of a chicken."

We'll close this chapter with a story about a very famous writer and speaker.

426. On one of his many lecture tours, Mark Twain realized that he needed a haircut, so he went to a barber shop. The following dialogue ensued:

Barber: "You picked a good time to come, stranger. Mark Twain's going to lecture tonight."

Twain: "He is? That's interesting."

Barber: "I suppose you'll go?"

Twain: "Oh, I guess so."

Barber: "Have you got a ticket?"

Twain: "Not yet."

Barber: "Then you'll have to stand. Everything's sold out."

Twain: "How annoying! I never saw such luck! I always have to stand when that fellow lectures."

And so on to the next chapter.

14.

Signs, Ads, Warnings, Headlines—and Brief Nonsenses

It's difficult to decide how to organize the bits and pieces that comprise this chapter. Perhaps we should start with total nonsense.

427. At the bottom of the menu in a restaurant in Fort Bragg, California, the owner had printed the following: "These items may or may not be available at all times and sometimes not at all and other times all the time."

428. A restaurant advertised: "Buy one hot dog for the price of two and receive a second hot dog absolutely free."

429. The business card of an eatery in Decatur, Texas, reads:

MATTIE'S

* * *

RESTAURANT AND YOGURT PARLOR
"An Alternative to Good Eating"

430. A friend of mine was driving through a medium-sized town and noticed four bakeries. Each had a different sign:

- The best Donuts in America!
- The best Donuts in the World!
- The best Donuts in the Universe!
- The best Donuts on this street.

She said that a local gas station attendant told her that the on-this-street bakery was doing the most business. An argument for prudence in advertising?

431. If you wonder why so many students these days are poor spellers, the following sign—all too typical—may explain it:

SUZI'S ALL-NITE E-Z
DRIVE THRU DONUT SHOPPE

432. Baking is an interesting and complex skill. This was especially well evidenced by a headline in the *Enquirer* of Battle Creek, Michigan. It read: IN-CLUDE YOUR CHILDREN WHEN BAKING COOKIES. (Perhaps I should have put this story in the chapter on "Families and Children.")

433. In Charlton, Massachusetts, there is a self-confident Chinese take-out restaurant called: KHANT GHO WONG.

434. A neighborhood was having a hot controversy over an ordinance that prohibited topless dancers in local bars. The owner of a fast-food chicken restaurant, seeing a good way to attract customers, posted a sign:

> NO NUDES HERE
> ALL OUR CHICKS ARE
> *TASTEFULLY* COVERED

435. If you think people are not passionate about different kinds of food, you don't know the people who live near the seaside near Boston. A local restaurant's menu had, among others, these two items:

New England clam chowder—$3.50 a bowl
$1.75 a cup

Manhattan clam chowder—Take Route I-95 south.

We won't take Route I-95 just now, but let's consider a few signs that drivers along roadways have read.

436. Perhaps this should come under "Government and Politics," but it's a long sign in small print posted just before the beginning of a winding, two-lane road. It was undoubtedly not an official sign. It read: "If you want to be a leader, just obey the 35-mile-an-hour speed limit for the next 10 miles."

437. As one approaches Orlando, Florida, a sign says:

> ENTERING ORANGE COUNTY
> (*not* from concentrate)

438. Two ignoramuses were on a trip from Michigan to Florida. They saw a sign that said: CLEAN REST ROOMS AHEAD. By the time they'd reached Florida they had cleaned twenty-eight rest rooms.

439. The English have a delightful way of giving warnings or directions:
- Sign in a country courtyard: DRIVE SLOWLY—CHILDREN AT LARGE
- Sign in a small church parking lot: PLEASE PARK PRETTILY

440. Another sign my wife and I saw beside a church in New Hampshire read exactly this way:

> CHURCH PARKING
> ONLY
> VIOLATORS
> TO WED
> AT THEIR OWN
> EXPENSE

I enjoy jotting down bumper stickers, except political ones. Here are some good ones:

441. When in doubt, read the book of instructions, the Bible.

442. God said it. I believe it. That settles it.

443. BE ALERT. America needs more lerts.

444. If you don't like the way I drive, get off the sidewalk.

445. Now that you mention it, I do own the road.

446. Brake for moose. The life you save may be your own.

447. Behind every schedule, someone is running.

448. Dirt is cheap—you have to dig for gold.

449. In Pennsylvania, cars have license plates only on the rear. Above the number, in small print, is written, "You've Got a Friend in Pennsylvania." But at some Christian bookstores for about $8, you can get a front license that reads:

> You've Got a Friend in
> # JESUS
> **PENNSYLVANIA**
> Never
> Expires   John 15:13–15

Here are more signs from various parts of the world—and the world beyond.

450. In a British golf club in Kenya, a sign at the first hole reads: "If the ball comes to rest in dangerous proximity to a crocodile or a hippopotamus, another ball may be dropped."

451. A jewelry store in the financial district of New York was having a tough time. They decided to take advantage of their situation and posted a large sign on the window: BUSINESS-STINKS SALE.

452. At another country church, this sign was posted on the door: "Brother Eben Cary departed for Heaven at 4:30 A.M."

Below the sign someone had written: "Heaven, 9 A.M. Cary not in yet. Great anxiety."

And so we come to various kinds of warnings, kind and not so kind.

453. Many joggers, dog exercisers, and bike-riding youngsters have worn a path across the grounds of a local church. However, the church—a kindly, welcoming institution—has posted a sign: "Trespassers will be forgiven—Matthew 6:14."

454. A less forgiving notice appears on a barn in Sullivan County, New York: "TRESPASSERS SHOT. IF MISSED, PROSECUTED!"

455. Sign in city council chambers of several cities: "NOT RESPONSIBLE FOR LOSS OF HATS, COATS, UMBRELLAS, OR TEMPERS."

456. In Bryn Mawr, Pennsylvania, there is an excellent hospital. However, in the parking area outside the emergency entrance there is a sign reading: "Parking for patients in labor only. Thirty-minute maximum."

A local commentator asked: "What, no special C-section rates?"

457. Sign in a doctor's waiting room: IS THIS YOU? "Oh, I feel good today, but every time I feel good I feel bad because I know I'm going to feel worse."

458. In Gastonia, North Carolina, there is a flourishing YMCA. Outside their basketball court a sign is posted: "Anyone caught hanging from the rim will be suspended."

459. Perhaps this story belongs in the chapter on "Marriage—a Complicated Human Condition." However, I place it under warnings. A woman bought a wig from a mail-order house. When the wig was delivered, the following note was enclosed: "Due to the possibility that this wig may slip off your head, do not wear it to bed. Many husbands have been frightened by the sudden awareness of a strange, furry animal under the blankets and have been known to damage the merchandise."

460. These warnings about damage to merchandise bring to mind those complicated, incomprensible instructions. Here's a set that's brief but incomprehensible. It comes on a product from Bulldog Home Hardware.

> TO OPEN:
> cut label slong
> dotted lines
> TO CLOSE:
> Lie flat on back &
> snap corners together.

Lie? Lay? See a good English handbook to have the distinction.

Now let's get back to signs: Here are a number that appear inside buildings or other structures—some seen by me, some sent by friends.

461. Outside a church: "I've had more trouble with myself than any other man I ever met."—American evangelist Dwight L. Moody (1837–1899).

462. Graffiti on a washroom wall at the Massachusetts Institute of Technology:

And God said:

$$\frac{mv^2}{r} = \frac{Ze^2}{r^2}$$

$$mvr = n\,\frac{h}{2\pi}$$

$$r = \frac{r^2 h^2}{(2\pi)^2\, mZe^2}$$

$$E = \tfrac{1}{2}mv^2 - \frac{Ze^2}{r}$$

$$E = \frac{2\pi^2 mZ^2 e^4}{n^2 h^2} = R$$

and there was light.

463. O.K. about God and M.I.T. How about this sign, observed by James B. "Scottie" Reston and reported in his great book *Deadlines*? During World War II, when he was in England, he saw this sign in Westminster Abbey: "In the event of an air raid, parishioners will descend to the crypts with all due reverent haste."

464. On the walls of the Sylvia Beach Hotel, Newport, Oregon, appear the following two signs:

• MAN WHO SAY A THING CANNOT BE DONE SHOULD NOT INTERRUPT WOMAN DOING IT.

- IF YOU DON'T KNOW WHERE YOU'RE GO-
  ING, ANY ROAD WILL GET YOU THERE.

465. In Big Sur, California, a friend tells me there are some Henry Miller Memorial Rest Rooms. Two quotations from Miller that are posted there:

- To relieve a full bladder is one of the great human joys.
- No harm can ever be done a great book by taking it with you to the toilet.

466. A then little-known U.S. Representative from Texas had a sign on his office wall that read: "You ain't learnin' nothin' while you're talkin'." The Representative was Lyndon Baines Johnson (1908–1973). Johnson exemplified this pronouncement so well that a staff member of his said, "Johnson listens so hard, it is deafening."

467. An earlier public figure, Henry Adams (1838–1918), was a well-known writer and historian. A saying of his is posted on a number of office walls in Washington: "Chaos often breeds life, when order breeds habit."

And this brings us back to signs—and business.

468. A window glass repair shop in Plymouth, New

Hampshire, sports this sign: "Every crack is a break for us."

469. A small Laundromat in Vermont uses a special sign to attract business: "Cleanest Wash in Town. Best Gossip."

470. A successful building contractor posted this motto in front of the premises: "Excuses are the nails used to build a house of failure."

471. Are you ever suspicious of slogans like: "Serving Philadelphia since 1802"? Well, in front of a real estate agency is a sign that is totally honest—and appealing: "Serving Arizona Since June."

Now let's turn to notices and announcements.

472. A friend of mine sent me this notice. He did not say what business or agency it came from.

NOTICE TO PERSONNEL
RE: Notice Regarding Notices

Please notice this important notice about notices. You may have noticed the increased amount of notices for you to notice. We have noticed that some of the notices have been noticed. On the other hand, some of our notices have not been noticed.

This is very noticeable. It has been noticed that the responses to the notices have been noticeably unnoticeable.

Would you please notice the voting boxes at the bottom of this notice. Please check (x) in one of the notice boxes that you notice below.

( )YES, I notice notices

( )NO, I don't notice notices

THE NOTICE COMMITTEE
FOR NOTICING NOTICES

473. When my wife and I were canoeing down the Androscoggin River in New Hampshire in 1991, we stopped at a campground to eat our lunch. There, posted on a tree, was this notice:

> GREAT ANNUAL RUBBISH BATTLE AND
> GARBAGE ENVIRONMENTAL RECOVERY

It was put up by the Androscoggin Riverbank Environmental Cleanup. Note the acronym made by the notice: GARBAGER

474. Here's an announcement from that noble place of learning, Harvard. It was published in the *Harvard Gazette*:

Dec. 17—Sponsored by the Winthrop House Music Society, the Beaux Arts Trio will perform

Zemlinsky's Trio in D minor, Op. 3, Schubert's Trio in E flat Minor, Op. 100, and a work to be announced by Mozart at 8 P.M. in Sanders Theatre.

If long-dead musicians can announce, it may well be that recently dead churchgoers can eat.

475. In Livonia, Michigan, there is a United Methodist church. It publishes the *Newburg Scroll*. In one issue it said: "Newburg Church tries to assist in serving a luncheon for the families of church members who have died immediately following the funeral."

As already shown here and there in this chapter, advertisements can be amusing, sometimes on purpose, sometimes unknowingly. Here are five ads that are, I suspect, unknowingly humorous.

476. This appeared in *The Daily*, newspaper of the University of Washington, Seattle:

HOUSEHOLD GOODS

AUTHENTIC COFFIN—used in theatre productions. Great novelty item for the dead.

477. In the *Minneapolis Tribune*:

FERRARI

25,986 ACTUAL MILES

WOW!! FERRARI red with buckskin leather.
1984 308 GTSi QV, 1 owner with removable top.

478. In the *South China Morning Post*, Hong Kong:
A dynamic mineral trading company has the following immediate position.

FEMALE ASS MERCHANDISER

—Minimum two-year experience in commercial
trading

—Able to handle all I/E documents

—Fluent English and Mandarin

479. Florence Nightingale Graham (1884–1966)
moved from Canada to New York City in 1909. She
worked as a secretary but soon got interested in pro-
moting beauty products for women. She changed her
name to Elizabeth Arden. Whether or not she would
have approved of the following promotion statement,
I don't know, but here's what the company said recently about Elizabeth Arden Ceramide Time Complex Capsules: "Take your skin back in time to the
future of a younger tomorrow."

480. The French Army was having a campaign to re-
cruit paratroopers. On one of the busiest streets in
Paris they placed their poster:

YOUNG MEN!

Join the parachutist forces
of France. It is more

dangerous to cross this
street than to jump
with a parachute.

The poster was a great success until someone scribbled at the bottom: "I would gladly join, but the recruiting office is on the other side of the street!"

481. Parachuting is not the only hazardous occupation. This headline appeared recently in a Phoenix paper: OUTSIDE CONSULTANT SOUGHT FOR TEST OF GAS CHAMBER.

482. We saw this poster in a public building: "If you must smoke, do not exhale."

483. In Corpus Christi, Texas, someone has posted on the crosswalk of Ocean Drive: "To cross Ocean, push button, wait for walk sign."

484. Another sign: "Welcome to Alabama—Drop in anytime!" This sign can only be seen by people who are dropping by parachute—probably from the Army's paratroop school near Columbus, Georgia.

485. Another bumper sticker: HONK IF YOU'RE A MORON WHO OBEYS BUMPER STICKERS.

486. An advertisement in the *Newport News*: "Treadmill $100, stair-stepper $75, mini trampoline $10, Thigh Master $10, crutches $10."

487. Imogene, Iowa, is a town of about 80 people. It has a magazine titled *The Imogene Hub* that ran this headline recently. IMOGENE ZOO CLOSES. The complete story followed, thus: "The chicken died."

488. A report in a Rochester, Pennsylvania, church bulletin: "The outreach committee has enlisted 25 visitors to make calls on people who are not afflicted with any church."

489. The following classified ad appeared in the West Branch, Michigan, *Northland Ad-Liner*: "Two male strippers looking for work. We take it all off from your chest to your drawers. Furniture stripping, repairing, and refinishing."

490. Sign on a clothing store in Boston's fashionable Newbury Street: WE HAVE BUTTON-FLY LEVI'S. OPEN TILL 10 TONITE.

491. Notice in a parish magazine: "It would be a

great help towards keeping the churchyard in good order if others would follow the example of those who clip the grass on their own graves."

492. A friend of mine went into a fast-food eatery and found this notice posed on each table: "If your order is not satisfactory, please return the product to the counter and we will replace it with a smile."

More bumper stickers:

493. GET EVEN! GROW OLD ENOUGH TO BE A PROBLEM TO YOUR CHILDREN

494. DON'T DRINK AND DRIVE. YOU MIGHT HIT A BUMP AND SPILL YOUR DRINK.

495. IF YOU LOVE ANIMALS, HUG A FOOT-BALL PLAYER

Even—or perhaps especially—churches use advertising.

496. On a bulletin board outside a church there was a sign that read: "If you have troubles, come in and tell us about them. If you have none, come in and tell us how you do it."

That sign might do just as well outside the office of an underemployed psychiatrist. However, be that as it may, it leads nicely into the next chapter.

15.

Religion—Con or Pro

I should be frank about myself at the start of this chapter. I'm a member of the Religious Society of Friends (Quakers), many of whom are not very "religious," in the narrow sense of the word. Perhaps the most appealing pronouncement of Quakers was that of its founder, George Fox (1624–1691), who said, "Thou shalt walk cheerfully over the world, answering that of God in every one." I would rather say, "answering that of love in every one," but I can't change George Fox. He's dead. I also like the statement "God is love" (Bible, 1 John 4.16). And the chapter goes on to say: "and he [she] that dwelleth in love dwelleth in God, and God in him [her]." But I'd prefer to say quite simply, "Love is love." *That*, I can believe in!

I also believe that religion—and the history, facts, and myths of religions—are great sources of humor. And so are churchgoers, ministers, and even the Pope. If you can't laugh at something (no, *with* something), it's not worth much—and religion *is*, no matter how many crimes have been (and are being) committed in its name.

But enough of all this serious talk! Let's get real—and please don't be offended.

497. An ancient f(F)riend of mine sent me this list of "Religious Truths." They all have to do with the word *shit*, which used to be a perfect, accurate description of bodily excrement. What do various world religions think about shit?

- *Taoism:* Shit happens.
- *Confucianism:* Confucius say, "Shit happens."
- *Buddhism:* If shit happens, it is not really shit.
- *Zen Buddhism:* What is the sound of shit happening?
- *Hinduism:* This shit has happened before.
- *Islam:* If shit happens, it is the will of Allah.
- *Protestantism:* Let shit happen to someone else.
- *Catholicism:* If shit happens, you deserve it.
- *Judaism:* Why does shit always happen to us?
- *Quakerism:* Shit?
- *Atheism:* Bullshit!

This leads nicely into a riddle.

498. *Question:* Who was the most constipated man in the Bible?

Answer: Moses (13th century B.C.), because he took two tablets and went up the mountain.

499. And here is another Bible riddle:

Question: Who was the Bible's greatest orator?

Answer: Samson, because he brought the house down even though it was filled with his enemies.

Let us now turn from riddles to prayers.

500. Spencer Coxe's wife was going to have a baby. In order to prepare his young son, Theodore, he asked, "Theo, would you like to have a little sister?"

"Oh, yes!" said Theo.

"Well, then," said Mr. Coxe, "start to pray for a sister."

Theo did this for a couple of weeks, but nobody came, so he got disgusted and quit.

A couple of days later Mrs. Coxe delivered twins, and Coxe took Theo to the hospital. He showed the boy the room and took him around to one side of the bed and showed him a baby girl. Then he took Theo to the other side of the bed and showed him another baby girl.

"Isn't that fine, Theo?" said the father. "What do you have to say?"

Theo replied, "The only thing I can think of to say is that I bet you're real glad I stopped praying."

501. The story is told that one day a priest came out of St. Patrick's Cathedral and saw a taxi driver trying to get a flat tire off the rim of a wheel. The driver was swearing loudly. Said the priest, "My son, please do not use the name of the Lord in vain."

"But I can't get this tire off," said the driver.

The priest said, "Here, let me take a look. Maybe I can help."

With that, he knelt down and prayed. A miracle happened, and the tire came off the rim. The priest was amazed and said, "Well, I'm a Goddamned son of a bitch!"

Here's a story about a special kind of prayer—saying grace before a meal.

502. For supper or any major meal, my wife and I always "say grace," a Quaker grace, by holding hands in silence for a moment before starting to eat. We've always done this with our children and also our grandchildren. Years ago, our youngest child, Emily, now a mother of two, was in her early teens. When we held hands and then gave a squeeze to show that grace was over, she often would object: "But you didn't give me time to finish my paragraph."

And now back to prayer away from the table.

503. The tendency of the Irish to engage in violent conflicts, Protestant against Catholic, is well-known, complicated, and often exaggerated. However, it caused one Irishman, probably with a good Irish twinkle in his eye, to pray: "O Lord, please make all

Irishmen into atheists. Then we shall be able to live together like Christians."

504. A storm was raging at sea, and the captain saw that his small ship was sinking. He called over the roar of the waves, "Does anyone aboard know how to pray?"

One sailor stepped forward and said, "Aye, Captain, I know how to pray."

"Good," said the captain. "You pray while the rest of us don our life jackets. You see, we're one jacket short."

505. For centuries Jews have been coming to the ancient Wailing Wall in Jerusalem to pray and recall their suffering.

Some time ago, two Jews met at the Wall. Both were very sad: One wailed—and prayed, "O God, have mercy upon me. My brightest son has become a Christian."

The second wailed, "O God, my *only* son has become a Christian."

And they both prayed for help.

God answered: "My only son has done the same."

The following story also deals with the age-old question of whether Jesus was a Jew.

506. *Questioner:* "Was Jesus a Jew?"

Person questioned: "There's no doubt about it—yes!"

Questioner: "How can you be so sure?"

Person questioned: "Look at the facts. He lived with his parents till he was thirty-two. He took over his father's business. He thought his mother was a virgin. And his mother thought he was God."

507. A totally unhistorical story, but one on the subject of *Was Jesus a Jew?*, is that of the Wise Man who hit his head on a low beam in the manger.

"Jesus Christ!" he exclaimed.

Mother Mary reacted positively. "I'm so glad you suggested that. We were going to call him Herman."

508. And of course, there is this classic tidbit on the subject:

> Roses are red,
> Violets are bluish.
> If it weren't for Jesus,
> We'd all be Jewish!

Preachers—at least almost all those I know—are hardworking, self-sacrificing, multichallenged, and yet joyful people. Here are a number of studies about them, many given to me by preachers themselves.

509. Mr. Henderson was the sort of man who went to

church for Easter and Christmas only. One Easter, to his amazement, he enjoyed the sermon. As he left the church, he said, "Reverend Samuel, that was a damn good sermon!"

Reverend Samuel: "Beg your pardon. I don't understand that kind of language."

Mr. Henderson: "That was such a damn good sermon that I put fifty dollars in the collection plate."

Reverend Samuel: "The hell you say! Thanks!"

510. A preacher in a West Virginia town was asking members for gifts to the church's program to buy food for the poor. The town gambler, who also owned a saloon and had made some shady real estate deals, offered the preacher $500.

A deacon of the church heard about the offer and was scandalized. "You can't take that!" he exclaimed. "That's the Devil's money!"

"Well, brother deacon," replied the preacher, "I see no harm in taking the money from the Devil and seeing what the Lord can do with it."

511. Wonderful as they are, preachers can't be perfect. In fact, some parishioners believe that no matter what they do, it's usually not quite right. As an example of this, a Catholic friend sent me the following:

WHO WILL REPLACE HIM?

If a priest preaches over ten minutes, he's long-winded.

If his sermon is short, he didn't prepare it.

If the parish funds are high, he's a businessman.

If he mentions money, he's money-mad.

If he visits his parishioners, he's nosy;

If he doesn't, he's being snobbish.

If he has fairs and bazaars, he's bleeding the people.

If he doesn't, there isn't any life in the parish.

If he takes time in confession to help and advise sinners, he takes too long.

If he doesn't, he doesn't care.

If he celebrates liturgy in a quiet voice, he's boring;

If he puts feelings into it, he's an actor.

If he starts Mass on time, his watch is fast.

If he starts late, he's holding up the people.

If he tries to lead the people in music, he's showing off;

If he doesn't, he doesn't care what the Mass is like.

If he decorates the church, he's wasting money;

If he doesn't, he's letting it run down.

If he's young, he's not experienced.

If he's old, he ought to retire.

But ... if he dies ...

THERE MAY BE NO ONE TO REPLACE HIM.

512. A preacher friend sent me this. I quote it exactly:

"A traveling evangelist always put on a grand finale at his revival meetings. When he was to preach at a church, he would secretly hire a small boy to sit in the ceiling rafters with a dove in a cage. Toward the end of his sermon, the preacher would shout for the Holy Spirit to come down, and the boy in the rafters would dutifully release the dove.

At one revival meeting, however, nothing happened when the preacher called for the Holy Spirit to descend. He again raised his arms and exclaimed: 'Come down, Holy Spirit!' Still no sign of the dove. The preacher then heard the anxious voice of the small boy call down from the rafters: 'Sir, a yellow cat just ate the Holy Spirit. Shall I throw down the yellow cat?' "

513. Preachers and priests are supposed to help their parishioners deal with their sins. I have never understood all of the categories of sin, but I do know that there are "seven deadly sins." These are sins that, if you do not confess and do penance for them, will send you to hell. The seven deadly sins (in Catholicism) are pride, covetousness, lust, anger, gluttony, envy, and sloth.

However, a non-Christian near-saint, Mohandas K. Gandhi (1869–1948), the great Indian politician and spiritual leader, had his own list of seven deadly sins: wealth without work, pleasure without conscience, knowledge without character, business without morality, science without humanity, worship without sacrifice, and politics without principle.

514. A preacher announced that there are 726 different kinds of sin. Almost at once he was besieged with requests for the list. He guessed the requests were mostly from people who thought they were missing something.

515. The great American Congregational preacher Henry Ward Beecher (1813–1887) had another view about sins. He said: "There are many persons who look on Sunday as a sponge to wipe out the sins of the week."

But back to sermons:

516. After church, two members were discussing the preacher's performance.

First member: "The sermon was divine. It reminded me of the peace of God. It passed all understanding."

Second member: "It reminded me of the mercy of God. I thought it would endure forever."

517. About fifty years ago there was a Friend in my Quaker Meeting in Germantown, Philadelphia, who had a tendency to speak frequently, lengthily, and incoherently, even though it was evident that he knew his Scriptures well. At last the overseers of the Meeting agreed that the next time he spoke, two members should usher him out.

The next Sunday, he did begin again to speak. After a few minutes, the two designated Friends arose and quietly walked over to him. They grasped him firmly by the elbows and propelled him toward the door. As they did, he looked around, glared at the worshipers, and shouted, "Our good Lord Jesus Christ rode into Jerusalem on the back of one ass. I am being carried out of Meeting on the arms of two."

518. A parishioner, who perhaps did not choose her words very carefully, told a preacher friend of mine: "You last sermon is always better than your next one."

519. Here is an interesting conversation between a young boy and his clergyman father. The boy was watching his dad write a sermon.

Boy: "How do you know what to say?"

Father: "Why, God tells me."

Boy: "Oh, then why do you keep crossing things out?"

520. A doctor friend of mine was telling a patient that he had high blood pressure and should take things easy. He then asked, "By the way, what do you do for a living?"

"I'm a preacher," the patient replied.

My friend commented, "That's exciting work. You exhort your flock and wave your arms, no?"

"Oh, no, Doc, I don't do any of that," the patient replied. "In fact, I only preach fifteen minutes."

"Well," my friend replied, "with your condition, that's plenty long enough."

With a look of confidentiality, the preacher said, "Actually, I only preach twelve minutes—and I allow three minutes for the enthusiasm!"

521. A new priest at his first Mass was so scared that he could hardly speak. After Mass he asked the Monsignor how he had done. The Monsignor said, "Fine, but next Sunday it might help if you put a little vodka or gin in your water glass to help relax you."

Next Sunday, the priest put some vodka in his glass and really talked up a storm. After Mass, he again asked the Monsignor how he had done. The Monsignor said, "Fine, but there are seven things we should get straightened out: One: There are ten Commandments, not twelve. Two: There are twelve disciples, not ten. Three: David slew Goliath; he did not kick the shit out of him. Four: We do not refer to Jesus Christ as the 'late J.C.' Five: Next Sunday, there is a taffy-pulling contest at St. Peter's—not a peter-pulling contest at St. Taffy's. Six: The Father, Son, and Holy Ghost are not referred to as 'Big Daddy, Junior, and Spook.' Seven, and last, the idea of a Drive-in-Confession was good, but the sign 'Toot and Tell or Go to Hell' has got to go."

522. Heinrich Heine (1797–1856), when asked on his deathbed whether God would forgive him: "Of course He'll forgive me. From this He makes a living."

523. The family dog produced a large litter of pups. Young Tom's parents said, "One dog is enough. Give the others away."

So Tom pondered and then a couple of Sundays later he showed up outside a local born-again Christian church. He was carrying a large cardboard carton labeled FUNDAMENTALIST PUPPIES. He did pretty well, but when everybody had gone there were still some puppies left.

The next Sunday he took his pup carton to a Quaker Meeting house. The label had been changed to: QUAKER PUPPIES. As he sat waiting for Friends to emerge from the meetinghouse, a woman walked by and saw the sign. She stopped, turned around, and said, "Young man, didn't I see you outside the fundamentalist church last week?"

"Yes, ma'am," replied Tom.

"And," said the woman rather sternly, "didn't your sign say they were fundamentalist puppies?"

"Yes, ma'am, it did," admitted Tom.

"Well, tell me," said the woman. "How did they go from being fundamentalist to being Quaker in just one week?"

Tom thought a moment and then replied brightly, "Ma'am, it's this way. Now their eyes are open."

524. Here's a special blessing: Blessed are they who engage in lively conversation with the helplessly mute—for they shall be called dentists.

525. And perhaps that's enough about preachers and sermons. Let's turn to the twelve apostles and a hypothetical memo that appeared in the November/December 1982 *Newsletter* of the Engineering Society, published in Gloucester, Ontario.

To:
Jesus, Son of Joseph
Woodcrafters Carpenter Shop
Nazareth 25922

From:
Jordan Management
Consultants, Jerusalem
26544

Dear Sir:

Thank you for submitting resumes of the twelve men you have picked for management positions in your new organization. All of them have now taken our battery of tests; and we have not only run the results through our computer, but also arranged personnel interviews for each of them with our psychologists and vocational aptitude consultant.

The profiles of all tests are included, and you will want to study each of them carefully.

As part of our service and for your guidance, we make some general comments. . . . It is the staff opinion that most of your nominees are lacking in background, education, and vocational aptitude for the type of enterprise you are undertaking. They do not have the team concept. We would recommend that you continue to search for persons of experience and managerial ability and proven capacity.

Simon Peter is emotionally unstable and given to fits of temper. Andrew has absolutely no qualities of leadership. The two brothers, James and John, sons of Zebedee, place personal interest above company loyalty. Thomas demonstrates a questioning attitude that would tend to undermine morale. We feel it is our duty to tell you that Matthew has been blacklisted by the Greater Jerusalem Better Business Bureau. James, son of Alphaeus, and Thaddaeus definitely have radical leanings, and both registered a high score on the manic-depressive scale. One, however, shows great potential. A man of ability and resourcefulness, he meets people well, has a keen business mind and contacts in high places, is highly motivated, ambitious, and responsible. We recommend Judas Iscariot as your controller and right-hand man. All other profiles are self-explanatory.

We wish you every success in your new venture.

526. An old Persian proverb says: "Trust in God, but tie your camel." Certainly many modern religious organizations seem to agree with this. For example, on a religious building in my neighborhood there are many noble mottoes posted, such as: TRUST IN GOD; HAVE FAITH IN THE LORD; JESUS IS OUR SAVIOR. However, equally prominent, although less elegantly inscribed, are several metal signs, especially near entrances. They read: SECURITY BY FRANKLIN BURGLAR ALARM, INC.

527. Woody Allen's view of religion goes something like this. He says: "Not only is there no God, but try getting a plumber on weekends."

Children have some interesting ideas about God and religion.

528. One of my grandchildren, Molly Eir Johnson Weisberg, is the daughter of a Quaker mother and a Jewish father. At age 3½ she was attending day-care at the Germantown Jewish Center, where much wonderful teaching is done about the Jewish religion, and on Sundays she attended Germantown Friends Meeting, of which she is a member.

Once when I was baby-sitting for her, we had a quiet moment and this exchange took place:

Gramps (me): "Molly, *where* is God?"

Molly (after pondering): "I don't know."

Gramps: "Well, Molly, *what* is God?"

Molly (with no hesitation): "Something Jewish."

529. Another grandchild, Laura Grace Mohler, at age 4½, was asked, "What is God?"

Without the slightest hesitation she replied, "A statue."

530. A mother who sends her child to parochial school reports that just before Christmas the sister told the story of the birth of Jesus. After she was done, she quizzed the children.

"What is baby Jesus' mother's name?"

"Mary! Mary!" they answered with enthusiasm.

"Good for you!" the sister said. "Now, what is baby Jesus' father's name?"

There was a thoughtful silence and then a small boy raised his hand. "I know, Sister!" he shouted. "It's Virg!"

"Virg?" the surprised nun asked.

"Yeah," explained the child. "You know—everybody's heard of Virg and Mary."

531. A five-year-old only child was playing with the small daughter of new neighbors. They were wading in the lake and finally decided that the only way to keep their clothes dry was to take them off.

They did so, and as they went back to the lake, the boy took a good look at the girl and said, "Gosh, I didn't know there was *that* much difference between Catholics and Protestants!"

532. A Catholic priest, a Protestant minister, and a Jewish rabbi were discussing the question of when life begins.

Priest: "Life begins at the moment of conception when the sperm and the egg unite."

Minister: "No, it begins when the fetus is viable, when if it should be born, it would be able to live."

Rabbi: "Well, my idea is that life really begins when the kids graduate from high school and go off to college."

533. Well, there are all sorts of religions, but maybe fewer than some people think. For example, a hotel clerk was amazed to see a guest walking through the lobby in his pajamas. He shouted, "Sir, what are you doing?"

The guest was startled and then said, "Oh, I beg your pardon. You see, I'm a somnambulist."

The clerk shouted again, "I don't care what your religion is. You can't walk around here like that."

534. In many parts of the United States church membership is declining. Perhaps that explains this large sign seen on the front of a church: THIS IS A CH–RCH. WHAT IS MISSING?

16.

Death, Heaven, Hell—
and Other Endings

You may be wondering why I'm ending a treasury of *humor* with a chapter on death, Heaven, and hell. Except possibly for Heaven, they don't seem like very humorous subjects. Well, I looked at the indexes of my two previous collections of humor, and I was surprised to find how many entries on these subjects there are.

A friend of mine, author John Keats (*not* the famous English poet), said, "Humor is the flip side of tragedy." That's worth thinking about. And George Bernard Shaw wrote: "Life does not cease to be funny when people die any more than it ceases to be serious when people laugh."

535. A favorite wise observation is that no one ever made it out of this world alive.

536. Mark Twain (1835–1910) made his opinion clear about life, death, and the afterlife when he said, "Heaven for the climate, hell for the company."

537. Thomas Hobbes (1588–1679), the great English philosopher, said when he knew he was dying at age 91, "I am about to take my last voyage, a great leap in the dark."

538. Samuel Butler (1835–1902), the English author, painter, and composer, whose best known work is *The Way of All Flesh* (1903), said, "Death is only a larger kind of going abroad."

And here are four more comments of death, in chronological order.

539. Marcus Antonius (121–180), a stoic philosopher: "Death, like birth, is a secret of nature."

540. George Santayana (1863–1952), Spanish-born American philosopher: "There is no cure for birth and death save to enjoy the interval."

541. James Thurber (1894–1961), American humorist:

Early to rise and early to bed
Makes a man healthy and wealthy and dead.

542. Sir Winston Leonard Spencer Churchill (1874–1965), British statesman, soldier, and author: "I am ready to meet my Maker. Whether my Maker is prepared for the ordeal of meeting me is another matter."

Here is another comment about death.

543. Headline in the *Register-Mail* of Galesburg, Illinois:

NURSING HOME PATIENTS
WHO ARE DEPRESSED
DIE MORE OFTEN

544. This leads us—if we believe in dying more than once—to Mark Twain's classic statement: "The reports of my death are greatly exaggerated." And Rudyard Kipling also lived to see his obituary mistakenly published in a newspaper. He wrote to the editor: "I've just read that I am dead. Don't forget to delete me from your list of subscribers."

545. George Bernard Shaw suggested the following

epitaph for himself: "I knew if I stayed around long enough, something like this would happen."

546. Speaking of epitaphs, Dr. Samuel Parr (1747–1825) was widely recognized as an excellent writer of epitaphs in Latin. Once he wrote to a noble British friend, "My Lord, should you die first, I mean to write your epitaph."

His friend replied, "Dr. Parr, it is a temptation to commit suicide."

547. Speaking of ways to death, I refer to John Wilkes (1727–1797), English politician and journalist. He once taunted the Earl of Sandwich by remarking: "I predict, sir, that you will die by hanging or from some loathsome disease."

The Earl replied, "That depends, my dear sir, on whether I embrace your principles or your mistress."

548. James Croll (1821–1890), the Scottish geologist and author, had never taken a drink in his life. As he was about to die, he asked for one, saying, "I don't think there's much fear of me becoming a drunkard now."

549. Then there are formal viewings of the body of a dead person. Mourners pay their respects to the deceased. One such mourner turned to the widow of the dead man and said, "Well, I must say Morris looks great!"

"So he should," replied the widow. "He just came out of the hospital."

Let's consider this marvelous opportunity to live on, long after you're dead.

550. In 1992 this ad appeared in *Yankee Magazine*:

"JUST THINK ... You passed away months ago ... and yet on every occasion that is important to those you left behind, and on their birthdays, they receive a BEAUTIFUL CARD expressing your warm and loving thoughts to them."

The ad was run by a company called Cards From Beyond in Fairport, New York. Before you die, you can arrange to have sent to your "loved ones" on specific annual occasions after your expiration, a beautiful card—for Thanksgiving, Christmas, and anniversaries, but not for Halloween. For example, the "Happy Birthday" card says: "On this special day of your life, take joy in the fact that those of us who have gone on before would give anything to be in your shoes."

The cost: $25 per card per year.

Thus we move nicely into the next section of this chapter: Heaven. According to a 1990 Gallup poll, 78%

of Americans believe in Heaven, and a 1991 Gallup poll shows that 91% of teenagers believe in afterlife. So it's a serious—and also a longtime humorous—subject.

551. Siddhārtha Gautama (ca. 563–ca. 483), more generally known as the Buddha, was asked by a disciple: "Is there life after death?"

"That question is unanswerable and pointless," the Buddha replied. He pointed to a fire burning nearby and asked, "Where was this flame before we kindled it?"

The disciple said, "I don't know. In some sense, the very question is not an accurate one. It didn't exist before."

The Buddha put out the flame and said, "Where is the flame now?"

Again the disciple said, "I don't know."

The Buddha ended the conversation saying, "Well, let's talk about things we do know."

What about getting into Heaven? Many people have a lot of fun with that question.

552. A reasonably religious physician friend of mine told me this story.

It happened that Ronald Reagan, Margaret Thatcher, and Mikhail Sergeyevich Gorbachev all died the same day and went to the Pearly Gates. Because of the importance of the arrivals, God was guarding the gates. Here's the dialogue:

God: "Ronald Reagan, why do you think you belong in Heaven?"

Reagan: "Well, I kept the peace for eight years and raised the spirits of the American people."

God: "Let me check the records. . . . Yes, you pass. Welcome!"

Gorbachev: "Well, I have fostered the restructuring of the Soviet Union, and worked for peace and openness."

God: "Let me check the records. . . . Yes, you have done good things. Come in!

"And now, Margaret Thatcher, why do you think you deserve to be in Heaven?"

Thatcher: "I consider your question to be irrelevant, and besides, you are sitting in my chair."

553. Wilson Mizner (1876–1933) was an American screenwriter and wit. Two of his remarks were: "All the movie heroes in Hollywood are in the audience"; and, speaking of death and Heaven: "Be nice to people on your way up because you'll meet 'em on your way down."

When Mizner was discussing his own death with a friend, he said, "When I die, I want a priest, a rabbi, and a Protestant clergyman. I want to hedge my bets."

554. William Camden (1551–1623), an English historian and schoolmaster, wrote:

A zealous locksmith died of late,
And did arrive at heaven gate,
He stood without and would not knock,
Because he meant to pick the lock.

555. The Reverend Paul R. Coleman of Zelienople, Pennsylvania, told the following story, which shows a delightful sense of humor and modesty about his own calling:

"A man and a woman who were friends for many years died and went to Heaven. They told Saint Peter they wanted to get married.

'Take your time and think about it,' Saint Peter said. 'You have an eternity to think about it here. Come back and talk to me about it in fifty years.'

Fifty years later, the couple returned and again told Saint Peter they wanted to get married.

'Take your time and think some more about it,' Saint Peter said. 'Come back and see me in another fifty years, and if we don't have a preacher up here by then, I'll marry you myself.' "

In our stories about Heaven, the subject of hell has sometimes been a part. Now here are four stories that are pure hell.

556. *Question:* What is a diplomat?

Answer: A man who can tell you to go to hell and make you look forward to the trip.

557. In the South after the Civil War when Union troops were still occupying Richmond, Virginia, an elderly lady slipped and fell while walking down a street. A Union soldier gallantly rushed to help her up. She glanced at his hated uniform and said, "Thank you very much, soldier. That's very kind of you." Then she smiled and continued. "If there's a cool spot in hell, I hope they give it to you."

558. A beach evangelist at a seaside resort was preaching loudly and denouncing his captive audience, all dressed in swimming costumes. He shouted, "Hell is full of drink, gambling, and loose women in suggestive bikinis."

At this point, a voice exclaimed from behind the sand dunes, "Oh, death, where is thy sting?!"

559. Perhaps this fourth story is not "pure hell"; it's more about the rehabilitation of a distressed area. It concerns an oilman from Texas who went to Heaven. Nice as it was, the Texan kept bragging about how in his state everything was even better. At last Saint Peter got weary and took the oilman to the edge of Heaven so that he could look straight down into hell.

Said Saint Peter, "Have you got anything like *that* in Texas?"

"No," the Texan replied, "but I know some ol' boys in Houston who can put it out."

Death, Heaven, hell—and *"Other Endings."* Some of the most delightful forms of "endings" are people's last words, or their epitaphs. Here are a number of them, arranged in chronological order.

560. Augustus (63 B.C.–A.D. 14), the first Roman Emperor (and grand-nephew of Julius Caesar): "Since well I've played my part, clap your hands, and with applause dismiss me from the stage."

561. François Rabelais (1494–1553), the French humanist and one of the great comic geniuses of literature, a doctor, and a Benedictine monk. His last will and testament was: "I owe much. I possess nothing. The rest I give to the poor."

562. Pietro Aretino (1492–1556), Italian poet, a great womanizer, and author of *Sonnets of the Lustful*. At his deathbed he regained consciousness and realized that a priest was giving him the last rites. His last words were: "Well, now that I am oiled, protect me from the rats."

563. Nicholas Boileau-Despreaux (1636–1711), a French poet who dared to say to Louis XIV, "Sire, nothing is impossible for Your Majesty. You set out to write some bad verses and you have succeeded," said at his death: "It is a great consolation to a poet on the point of death that he has never written a line injurious to good morals."

564. John Gay (1685–1732) was an English playwright and poet, best known for *The Beggar's Opera*, about thieves and prostitutes. He is buried in Westminster Abbey under an epitaph he wrote himself:

Life is a jest, and all things show it;
I tho't so once, and now I know it.

565. Lady Mary Wortley Montagu (1689–1762), an English author known mostly for her letters, led a full life and traveled widely. Her last words: "It has all been most interesting."

566. Oliver Goldsmith (1730–1773), the Anglo-Irish author of *She Stoops to Conquer* and *The Vicar of Wakefield*, was asked on his deathbed by a doctor, "Is your mind at ease?" His last words were, "No, it is not."

567. Georg Wilhelm Friedrich Hegel (1770–1831), great German philosopher: "Only one man ever understood me, and even he didn't understand me."

568. Heinrich Heine (1797–1856), whose best-known song is "Die Lorelei," was an avid writer. His last words were: "Write, write; pencil, paper."

569. John Greenleaf Whittier (1807–1892), devout Quaker and fierce opponent of slavery, said to friends gathered around his deathbed: "My love to the world."

570. Henrik Ibsen (1828–1906), Norwegian playwright whose works included *A Doll's House* (1879), *The Wild Duck* (1884), and *Hedda Gabler* (1890), was on his deathbed. The attending nurse said, "You seem to be improving." Ibsen replied, "On the contrary," and died.

571. Lytton Strachey (1880–1932), the English biographer and critic who wrote *Eminent Victorians* (1918) and *Queen Victoria* (1921), lay dying of stomach cancer. He said, "If this is dying, I don't think much of it."

572. Dylan Thomas (1914–1953), the Welsh poet who wrote the drama *Under Milk Wood*: "I've had

eighteen straight whiskeys. I think that's the record."
He then died.

573. B. P. Roberts (1929–1979), an unknown person,
buried in Mallory Square, Key West, Florida: "I told
you I was sick."

574. DeWitt Wallace (1889–1981), founder of the
Reader's Digest, suggested this epitaph for himself:
"The final condensation."

We've been considering items concerning the
end—or near the end—of life (other people's, of
course!). We're also approaching the end of this book,
and I've been trying to decide what its "last words" will
be. I hope to end on an optimistic note, but before that,
a couple of stories.

575. Mark Twain once went to a dinner party where
the chief subject of conversation was talk about eter-
nal life and future punishment, Heaven and hell.
Twain sat in silence throughout the conversation. Finally a woman asked, "Why do you not say anything? I would like to hear your opinion."

"Madam, you must excuse me," Twain replied. "I
am silent of necessity—I have friends in both
places."

576. Mark Twain again: "I believe that our Heavenly Father invented man because he was disappointed in the monkey."

577. The following remarks were made on March 14, 1992, by Andrew F. Sharpless, whom I taught at Germantown Friends School, at a reception after the Quaker wedding of his sister Laura, whom I also taught, to a Catholic: "I want to say a few words about religion. This is the second time for the Sharplesses that a Catholic and a Quaker have fallen in love and gotten married. So Beth and I want to welcome Tom and Laura to our special faith—Frisbeetarianism. We've found that despite our different backgrounds, we share certain beliefs as Frisbeetarians. As Frisbeetarians, we agree that when you die, your soul goes up on the roof and you can't get it down."

578. The following letter was received from Chase, P. O. Box 30700, Tampa, Florida:

Dear Mortgagor:

I wanted to make sure that you have a second opportunity to enroll in this excellent ACCIDENTAL DEATH AND DISMEMBERMENT PROGRAM. . . .

And the letter goes on.
Optimistic?

579. A friend and co-worker of mine on projects for
the good of Philadelphia, John Francis Marion, was a
lover of graveyards, around which he frequently gave
tours. When he died, it was discovered that he had
made up this epitaph for himself, the date of death inserted afterward:

> Curtain Call
> for
> John Francis Marion
> 1922–1991
> Who
> during Time's interval
> daily waylaid
> Eternity

580. "Other endings" can be hoped for long before
death, and so can Heaven on earth.

An English teacher told her senior class, "If you
want to succeed in the world, you must develop a
large vocabulary. Use a word ten times and it will be
yours for life."

In the back of the room a good-looking student
closed his eyes and was heard chanting under his

breath, "Beth, Beth, Beth, Beth, Beth, Beth, Beth, Beth, Beth, Beth."

581. H. L. Mencken (1880–1956), the pungent American essayist and author of the monumental *The American Language*, wrote his own epitaph: "If after I depart this vale, you ever remember me and have thought to please my ghost, forgive some sinner and wink your eye at some homely girl."

582. Charles Robert Darwin (1809–1882), who firmly established the theory of organic evolution and was the author of *Origin of Species*, was neither optimistic nor pessimistic about life. He wrote: "As for a future life, every man must judge for himself between conflicting vague probabilities."

So a great thinker asks you to judge for yourself. And as you judge, may humorous stories deepen and temper your judgment—and improve your life!

Life does have its problems, but some people, even—or perhaps especially—children, can look upon them with a positive eye.

583. A fourth-grade boy called his father into the backyard to show his dad his batting skills. He tossed a baseball into the air and swung mightily, but he missed.

"Wait, Dad," he said. "Watch this." He repeated the process a second time and swung even harder, but he missed again.

"Don't go, Dad," he said. "This is it." And he tossed the ball up for the third time, swinging his bat as before, but it was a third miss.

Undaunted, the youngster said to his father, "Three strikes and you're out. Gee, Dad, aren't I a great pitcher!"

So, dear reader, three strikes and you're *in*! So keep pitching, and keep sharing, humor and joy.

584. And consider the daily prayer a 93-year-old woman gave to her admired friend and pastor, Dr. Dale E. Turner, a Seattle, Washington, minister whose sermons are published in columns in *The Seattle Times*:

Come, thieving time, take
what you must,
Quickness to move, to hear, to
see,
When dust gathers near to
dust,
Such diminutions need must
be,
But leave, O leave, exempt
from plunder

My sense of humor, curiosity and wonder.

So, dear reader, laugh, question, and wonder! This book, and humor, can never say:

THE END

Index

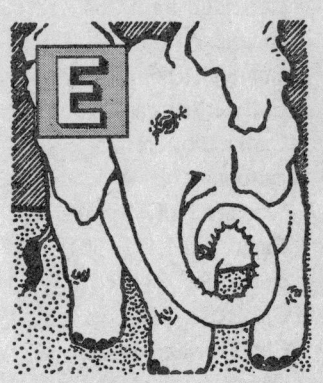

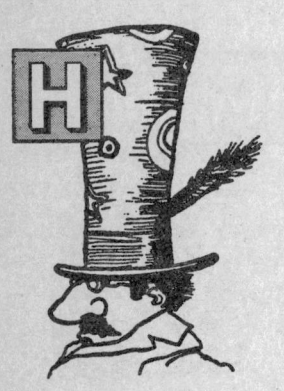